Always Rising

A SMALL-BUSINESS WOMAN TURNING SETBACKS INTO SUCCESS

Anissa Renae

First published by Ultimate World Publishing 2025
Copyright © 2025 Anissa Renae Kunda

ISBN

Paperback: 978-1-923583-08-5
Ebook: 978-1-923583-09-2

Anissa Renae Kunda has asserted her rights under the Copyright, Designs and Patents Act 1988 to be identified as the author of this work. The information in this book is based on the author's experiences and opinions. The publisher specifically disclaims responsibility for any adverse consequences which may result from use of the information contained herein. Permission to use information has been sought by the author. Any breaches will be rectified in further editions of the book.

All rights reserved. No part of this publication may be reproduced, stored in or introduced into a retrieval system, or transmitted in any form, or by any means (electronic, mechanical, photocopying, recording or otherwise) without the prior written permission of the author. Any person who does any unauthorised act in relation to this publication may be liable to criminal prosecution and civil claims for damages. Enquiries should be made through the publisher.

Cover design: Ultimate World Publishing
Layout and typesetting: Ultimate World Publishing
Editor: Gayle Oddy

Ultimate World Publishing
Diamond Creek,
Victoria Australia 3089
www.writeabook.com.au

Testimonials

Any woman in business will see parts of her own story in the pages of Renae's book. For those who are starting out, what a great way to understand how paths are forged.

Julia Spicer OAM, Goondiwindi

One of the great strengths of any entrepreneur is to be coachable. When Renae first came to our Meet the Press MasterClass, her pitch for the journos was about her business and the tourism industry. But when it came time to pitch to SmartCompany, I suggested something different – that she pitch how she and her husband had worked together for 30 years without killing each other! Initially unsure, Renae embraced the advice and secured not only a piece in SmartCompany, but one that generated over $50,000 in additional revenue. Many entrepreneurs would want to 'stick to their guns' and stick with their original pitch. Renae's ability to be coachable is one of the central qualities that have made her so successful – both behind the scenes and now in her own right. No entrepreneur journey is a straight line. It's been Renae's strength, resilience and resourcefulness that have all combined to make her the powerhouse she is today. She's nothing short of inspirational!!

Kate Englar, The Publicity Princess

Can I just say, I have always admired the woman you are, and in the past few years in particular, I have watched and read avidly your growth and the stories you've shared.

In the past 2-3 years, I have been pushing myself well outside of my comfort zone professionally and personally, learning how to be the leader I want to be. While I have attended courses, read books and articles, I feel I get so much more out of what you share, maybe because I know you personally to be a compassionate, hardworking and REAL person. You are someone worth admiring and aspiring to be more like. Thank you for sharing your stories, for being you and for being a woman I continue to look up to. I look forward to buying your book when it comes out. xx

Rebecca Fuller, Brisbane, QLD AUS

For 15 years, I've had the privilege of being a family friend to the author, and I've watched firsthand as she has faced immense challenges with incredible resilience, strength and grace. Her words are a powerful reflection of that experience, teaching me that 'opportunity belongs to the brave.' As a 'woman behind the man' in my own fledgling business, Renae's approach to conflict, connection and leadership resonated with me on a profound level. This book felt like a guiding story, whispered to me by a wise friend, to help me navigate the balance of business, innovation and creativity, while still being everything to everyone. It is an invaluable companion for anyone on a journey through the challenges of business, legacy and personal authenticity.

Georgia Holland, Townsville, QLD AUS

Dedication

For my children, my grandchildren and the generations to follow.

You are the reason I build. The reason I write. The reason I keep showing up when it's hard.

This book is more than a collection of stories. It's a record of grit, growth and the choices that shaped me. It's here to remind you that your voice matters, your story counts, and your path, however winding, is worth walking.

If anything in these pages helps you make sense of your own journey, then it's done its job.

You are the continuation of everything I've worked for. You are my most tremendous success in motion. And you are more than enough.

And to every woman who reads these pages, may you find the courage to see your own story as a success in motion.

With love and intention,

Mumma Grum xx

Contents

Testimonials	iii
Dedication	v
Introduction: Standing Up, Speaking Out and Building Something That Lasts	1
Chapter 1: Footprints in the Sand: A Childhood of Change	5
Chapter 2: From Haircuts to Horizons: Discovering My Path	13
Chapter 3: Human Revelations and New Beginnings	23
Chapter 4: Anchored in Connection: Lessons from the Sea	33
Chapter 5: Forgiveness and Fortitude: Balancing Life's Trials	45
Chapter 6: Knowledge Is Power: From Courtroom to Classroom	59
Chapter 7: Rebuilding Trust: From Betrayal to Empowerment	71
Chapter 8: Adventures and Adversities: Living the Dream	83
Chapter 9: Turning Challenges into Triumphs: Writing and Winning	99
Chapter 10: Love, Loss and Legacy: Finding Meaning in the Journey	113
Chapter 11: Rebuilding in Real Time: The Aftermath and the Anchor	127
Chapter 12: The Beginning of a New Chapter	139

Afterword: With Gratitude for Every Step	151
About the Author	153
Testimonials	155
Speaker Bio	159
Offers	161
Call to Action	163

Introduction

Standing Up, Speaking Out and Building Something That Lasts

For 35 years, I worked in the shadow of a tourism legend, quietly shaping a business that became a cornerstone of adventure tourism in Australia. But for most of that time, the congratulations didn't come to me; they went to my husband.

This isn't a complaint. It's the truth. And it's one I know thousands of women will recognise instantly.

In the male-dominated world of adventure tourism, I was the 'woman behind the man'. The one who made sure the wheels kept turning, the paperwork was filed, standards were met and the business kept growing. I was the one who translated my education, my experience and my instincts into real-world wins, only to see those wins credited to 'his' business. I didn't mind at first. I was proud of what we were building together. But over time, I started to realise that I wasn't just supporting a business; I was shaping a unique industry. And I wasn't just standing behind someone; I was standing in my own power, even if no one else saw it yet.

For years, I joked that my career was 'making tick boxes on forms.' It was my way of minimising the big feelings I didn't know how to express. Because behind that joke was a more profound truth: I was creating the very standards our industry would come to recognise and repeat. When we started, there was no roadmap for what we were doing. No guidelines. No recognition. We had to fight for every tick box, every certification and every nod of legitimacy. And I was the one doing the fighting.

At 50, something shifted. After decades of quiet contribution, I watched as multiple new businesses entered our industry and tried to claim recognition for the work we'd pioneered years earlier. One small sentence sparked a moment of clarity. In that moment, I realised I had a choice: continue in the shadows or step into my own light. I chose to stand up and be counted. To let my voice be heard. Not because I was angry and not because I wanted credit, but because I had something to say. I had learned a few things. I had walked the hard path. And I knew that if I could share what I'd learned, maybe I could make someone else's journey a little easier.

This book is for the women who walk a similar path. Those who stand in the shadows of great men, quietly trying to build a legacy, without any recognition. Those who want to make magic happen behind the scenes, who are holding the family together while running the business. Those who create order out of chaos and call it 'just helping out.' I see you. I've been you. And I want you to know that your work matters.

It's also for the small business owners who are building something bigger than profit. Something deeper than a brand. Something that will last. Because success isn't something you can buy or find; it's something you build, one step at a time. It's in the way you treat your customers, the way you lead your team, the way you show up when things get hard. It's in the values you live by, the dreams you bring to life and the stories you leave behind.

Over the years, I've collected many stories. Some are wild, some are funny, and some are downright unbelievable. But each one taught me something. Each one shaped the way I lead, the way I serve and the way I show up in the world. And now, I'm ready to share them.

This book isn't a how-to guide. It's about resilience, adaptability, courage and the quiet, often invisible work of building something that lasts. It's a reflection on the lessons I learned the hard way and a celebration of the success I'm still building: my second chapter. I hope that these stories will resonate with you, make you laugh, make you think and maybe even make you feel a little less alone.

I've called it *Always Rising* because that's what life and business truly are: a series of small steps that add up to something remarkable. And by the end, I'll share how this philosophy has grown into not just *my* story but a community of like-minded business owners who stand together and create their own success.

Because if there's one thing I've learned, it's that we're all walking each other home. And if my journey can help soften yours or make it just a little bit easier, then every tick box I ever created will have been worth it.

So, to the women in the shadows, the small business owners with big hearts, the builders behind the scenes: this book is for you. Let's turn those setbacks into success – together.

Chapter 1

Footprints in the Sand: A Childhood of Change

'A father holds his daughter's hand for a short while, but he holds her heart forever.' – Unknown

My earliest memory is from the day before my third birthday, when I was a flower girl at my aunt's wedding. Dressed in a pink satin gown, I felt like a princess until the grandeur of the day overwhelmed me, and all I wanted was my dad. That moment, and many others, taught me the power of love and security – constants that shaped every chapter of my life.

Growing up, I was surrounded by an enduring sense of love and security that became a constant in every chapter of my life. It wasn't until I started school that I realised being an only child was considered unique. Despite that, I never felt alone. With a large extended family of aunts, uncles, cousins and all 4 of my grandparents, I felt incredibly fortunate to be part of such a loving and connected family.

That foundation of safety and belonging shaped me more than I realised at the time. In business, we often underestimate the power of stability; whether it's a secure team, strong family values or simply knowing someone has your back. Yet the businesses that thrive are usually those with strong roots. For me, those roots were planted early in life, within my family, through rituals and in stories.

When I was just one year old, Cyclone Althea tore through Townsville, destroying my parents' first home. The howl of the cyclone was deafening, a sound so primal it seemed to shake the very air. Glass shattered, wind roared, and debris battered the house like a relentless drumbeat. On that chaotic day, I was toddling behind my dad down the hallway when he paused, picked me up, stowed me safely into my cot and then continued his storm patrol of the house. Moments later, a plate-glass window shattered, sending shards flying into him. The glass tore into his forehead and pierced his entire right side, leaving him badly injured and bleeding.

FOOTPRINTS IN THE SAND: A CHILDHOOD OF CHANGE

In the absence of emergency services, my mum became our sole lifeline. She quickly wrapped my dad in towels, helped him to the car and buckled me into a flimsy 70s-era car seat. By the time we arrived at the hospital, the car's blue paint had been stripped to bare silver by the storm's violent and powerful winds, as well as the relentless barrage of erosive debris they carried. It was a vivid reminder of the sheer force of a cyclone and the destruction it can bring.

How on earth she made it to the hospital we will never know, but my mind conjures countless images of what it must have been like for her that day. My dad was groaning in pain, and his blood would have been a scary sight, adding to the chaos of the storm raging outside. Thankfully, her experience as a 'candy striper' had given her some basic nursing knowledge, but I imagine it was the sounds that were most terrifying. The howl of a cyclone is unlike anything you can imagine until you've lived through one. My mum's calm decisiveness in the chaos became a lesson I would carry for life: when the storm rages, your response defines the outcome.

The silver lining of the disaster was that I was the only baby on the block, which meant my parents were granted a larger allowance of ice for beer, and the family and neighbours stopped by every day. The cyclone left my dad with a distinct, arched scar on his forehead, a unique mark that set him apart from everyone else, a natural conversation starter. Strangely, he never seemed the least bit bothered by it.

My dad was a striking young man, very James Dean, confident and proud. So why wasn't this noticeable blemish a source of annoyance for him? My dad also had a vivid imagination. That scar wasn't just a scar; it was the mark of a tiger attack or the result of a brush with an elephant's tusks, at least according to his stories. Whenever my child-self got bored, I would simply ask Dad what had happened, and he would take me on a grand and perilous adventure in which he always came out victorious. It wasn't until

I was an adult that I learned the truth behind it. I think he liked the mystery the scar created, the way it invited curiosity and allowed him to spin a new tale each time someone asked. It wasn't just a mark; it was a gateway to storytelling, and he embraced it fully.

The author's father – Circa 1960s

Business reflects life; storms come in many forms. Some are literal, such as floods, fires and pandemics. Others are more metaphorical, like financial downturns, sudden staff departures or a key client walking away. You can't control the storm, but you can choose how you respond. My mum's calm decisiveness has guided me throughout my life, and it's the same mindset that steadies a business during a crisis. Likewise, our scars aren't flaws; they're stories. They create connections. In business, our failures, close calls and hard-earned lessons often attract others to us. Instead of hiding them, we can use them as bridges to trust.

FOOTPRINTS IN THE SAND: A CHILDHOOD OF CHANGE

Losing the house led us to start fresh in Mackay. Mum left her parents and 4 sisters behind, while Dad joined my uncle's (his brother-in-law's) building company. Together, they played a key role in shaping Mackay, building 100 houses in that first year alone. It was just the 3 of us going through this new chapter.

As I got older, I began to understand the struggles my parents faced behind the scenes, even though they never showed it. Both were hardworking and committed to their full-time jobs. My mum worked in administrative roles, while my dad was a plasterer, carefully shaping the walls and cornices of someone's new home. Their workplaces became special places for me as a kid. I remember visiting the carpet store where Mum worked and being amazed by the dark storeroom filled with huge rolls of carpet; it felt like exploring the pyramids, to my young imagination. At my dad's work, leftover plaster and spare boards became my art space. I would make messy masterpieces, but my favourites were always my handprints pressed into the plaster. It was just like staring in awe at 'Winged Victory' in the Louvre.

We would live in one of these houses built by my uncle's business for a while, but whenever Mum decided the ceiling needed cleaning, we'd simply move on to the next build. Mum was so adept at this game that she kept paper replicas of our furniture in a pencil case, scaled to size that would fit on a page in a graph book. Ultimately, they achieved their goal of owning a house and paid cash for the final house they built.

My poor mother had her hands full with the 2 of us. She worked a 9-to-5 job, came home to cook dinner every night and spent her weekends washing and cleaning, like the generations of women before her. There was little time for indulgence during the week, so steak and 3 vegetables were staples on our dinner plates. But weekend meals were different; we'd often spend time at barbecues with friends, and everyone would contribute something to the meal. Mum would spend hours in the kitchen creating magic in the form of her unforgettable peach blossoms or a Flake and cream cheesecake that seemed otherworldly. My mum was beautiful, and I cherished watching her get ready to go out. She would carefully apply her lipstick and twirl in front of the mirror, seeking that final moment of self-approval, as I secretly admired her.

She was also incredibly skilled with a sewing machine, a talent I took for granted at the time. She made costumes for school plays and crafted beautiful new outfits for me. While other girls were wearing hand-me-downs, I was dressed in unique, handmade creations that made me feel both special and glamorous. Looking back, I now see just how talented and extraordinary she truly was as a mother.

On Saturdays, Dad and I were often kicked out of the house, and we'd usually end up at the beach. I'd trail behind him, carefully placing my feet in his winding, wide, or very narrow, or circular footsteps in the sand. He'd glance back, chuckling as I furrowed my brow, trying to match his steps, sometimes tripping over my own feet. The game always ended with a big leap, and his quiet laughter echoed over the waves to reach my heart. Afterwards, we'd sit together, gazing out to sea and watching the birds glide across the horizon.

The footprints we leave behind become guides for those who follow us.

I was Dad's partner-in-crime; he'd instigate and drag me along for the ride. His inner prankster personality was the opposite of his outer, stern and responsible persona. Mum was our warden; she kept everything running smoothly. She made sure we had a steady routine, a clean home and full bellies. Sunday nights were her least favourite part of the week but one of my fondest memories. That was sheet-changing night.

FOOTPRINTS IN THE SAND: A CHILDHOOD OF CHANGE

As we dragged tiredly through the last fragments of the weekend, the moment came when the fresh sheet would billow up, ready to settle perfectly on the bed. Just before it landed, Dad would swoop in from nowhere, ducking under the parachute and roaring like a jet engine. Mum would let out an exasperated scream while I dissolved into laughter. This playful chaos wasn't a one-time act; it was a ritual, repeated at least 10 times every Sunday night for my amusement.

Even when Mum didn't ask for help, Dad found a way to join in. He'd launch himself onto the bed from angles no one expected, consistently beating the sheet to its landing and driving Mum to a hilarious performance of fake frustration. Watching them play this silly little game every week, I understood that this teasing was their love, expressed in the quirkiest, most endearing way.

Because we moved house so often, I attended 9 schools in 10 years, constantly the new kid walking into tight-knit classrooms. It wasn't easy, but it taught me how to adapt, project confidence and build connections quickly – skills that became invaluable in business.

Growing up as an only child with parents who both worked full-time made school holidays a bit of a challenge. To solve this, my parents would fly me to Townsville to stay with my grandparents and aunts. My grandmother, who ran a kindergarten for 40 years, created the perfect environment for young children. She was a woman of strict routines; every day followed the same precise order from early dawn until she collapsed into bed well after dusk. Her unwavering discipline extended to everyone around her. You either followed her rules or got swept aside. She didn't waste time, but when she allowed herself to play, her warmth and joy would shine through. Those moments were rare, but they were worth waiting for.

My favourite part of the kindy day was music class, just before lunch. My grandmother was incredibly musical, playing the piano and singing nursery rhymes with a passion that we all adored. When she was at the piano, every child loved her. But we also knew better than to cross her. Her 'cranky voice' was legendary, and none of us dared misbehave in her presence.

By the time I turned 7, I was already weary of being labelled an 'unaccompanied minor' on flights. I was embarrassed to have the tag pinned to my clothes, and I didn't need a flight attendant to escort me across the tarmac; I was perfectly capable of handling it myself. I knew how to buckle a seatbelt, read the safety card and follow instructions without assistance. Yet, waiting on the plane long after everyone else had disembarked felt unbearable, especially knowing my grandmother was waiting for me and my holiday was being needlessly delayed for unrequired adult assistance.

In hindsight, those early travel experiences ignited my enduring love for exploration and taught me valuable lessons. From mastering the art of navigating airports to cherishing moments with family, those childhood journeys played a significant role in shaping the person I am today.

These early lessons – resilience, storytelling, adaptability, discipline and ambition – weren't just family memories. They were the foundation of my entrepreneurial DNA. And they remind me that success doesn't start with a business plan; it starts with the footprints we leave behind.

REFLECTION QUESTIONS FOR YOU:

Think back to your own childhood. What early experiences shaped the way you face challenges today? How can you use those lessons as part of your business story?

Chapter 2

From Haircuts to Horizons: Discovering My Path

'I was not a wild child, but I did rebel. And now I look back and see that rebellion was my way of asking for love, for space, for truth. I forgive her, the girl I was, because she was trying to become.' – Unknown

Attending 9 schools in 10 years meant my childhood unfolded in a constant whirl of new faces, classrooms and playground rules. As an only child, I didn't have siblings to teach me life's lessons. Instead, I learned them the hard way, through the eyes of adults and the sharp edges of childhood cruelty.

My height gave me a slight edge, helping me avoid most physical bullying, but harsh words were everywhere. Why are kids so cruel to each other? I was an average student, easily distracted, and my report cards always mentioned my habit of talking during class instead of listening. Nothing has changed there; my biggest challenge remains listening before I speak.

School life felt ordinary until I set my sights on something unexpected: a Catholic girls' high school. Despite not being Catholic and having always attended public schools, I was determined. I was only 9 when I made this decision, and even now, it feels strange. The best way in, I discovered, was to spend 2 years at a Catholic primary school, so I switched the following year.

This was no small request of my father. He wasn't religious, quite the opposite. As I got older, I began to see the prejudices he held against religion, race and creed. While I loved him deeply and he remained my superhero, I started realising that people didn't always hold lovely or fair opinions about humanity. These small observations would become clear 'aha' moments much later in life.

Every morning, I felt the relief of slipping into a uniform, not having to agonise over what to wear. Even now, I cherish the freedom of lounging at home in pyjamas, free from daily outfit dilemmas. There's wisdom in this simplicity. I've heard that Einstein owned 7 identical suits to conserve his mental energy for more important matters. Whether true or not, the principle holds: when you reduce unnecessary decisions, you create space for creativity and problem-solving. In business, uniforms, branding and systems all serve the same purpose: they simplify choices and free up mental space for the real work.

Those school years weren't easy, especially when it came to fitting in. A nun I'll call Sister A made it painfully clear that I didn't belong because I wasn't Catholic. At just 10 years old, her coldness stung, not just because it was unfair but because it made me question my place in a world that seemed to favour others over me.

One particular day remains vivid. We were standing in line, waiting to return to class. It was summer in the Far North, and I was right next to the water bubbler. Feeling thirsty, I leaned over for a quick sip. Out of nowhere, Sister A raced up behind me and smacked me hard across the shoulder, causing my teeth to hit the steel frame.

Her coldness taught me something fundamental: bias has a way of sneaking out. It colours behaviour, influences decisions and impacts lives. Sister A may not have admitted her prejudice, but I carried the bruise of it. Years later, I realised this lesson shaped how I chose to lead. Unconscious bias happens just like that: clients are favoured or overlooked and employees promoted or ignored, not always for their merit but because of someone else's hidden bias. Fairness isn't automatic; it's a deliberate choice.

The church at the edge of the playground became a sacred hideaway for my best friend T and me. We'd meet there before school, drawn to its vast stillness and the quiet play of shadows. Dust particles danced in beams of coloured sunlight streaming through stained-glass windows – pure enchantment. Our footsteps echoed softly, and though we tried to keep our voices low, giggles always built up.

Father X discovered us there one morning and started joining us occasionally. He even took us up the bell tower a few times – something strictly forbidden by Sister A, which made us feel special and rebellious. That changed the day I was told I couldn't join them anymore; apparently, the bell tower was only for Catholics. T was invited without me, and I had to return to the school grounds alone.

She'd come back crying, refusing to tell me why, until she stopped wanting to go altogether. She got sick when we had to attend church with our class. At the time, I couldn't understand it. Years later, when headlines broke about paedophile priests, my stomach filled with grief, relief, shock and anger. I finally understood what those silent signals meant and how my lovely, happy friend lost her spark in just a few months.

Not everyone will walk with you into the light. Some cling to the shadows, and you must let them.

High school brought the usual mix: first boyfriends, heartbreaks, body shame and learning to sift truth from lies. It all felt routine until work experience week came around. Suddenly, we were thrust into the 'real world', expected to perform and adapt.

My dream was to become a racehorse trainer, just like my dad, who had stables in the backyard and horses as a hobby, but that wasn't an available work experience opportunity. Following most girls in my year, I put down 'hairdresser' as my second choice. My mum arranged a placement at a salon near her office.

That week opened a whole new world, offering a glimpse of what adulthood might hold. I fell in love with the creative energy, the sense of responsibility and the little freedoms that came with 'big girl shoes'. The magic of having a job, something that belonged solely to me, was unforgettable. By the end of the week, my boss offered me a position to start when school finished.

FROM HAIRCUTS TO HORIZONS: DISCOVERING MY PATH

Suddenly, school days dragged. I felt out of step, itching for what was next. When neighbourhood friends decided to skip their sports day, I gave in to temptation and joined them. What started as innocent fun escalated when someone dropped a lit cigarette in the cane fields, and the dry undergrowth exploded into flame.

The party scattered, but I stood out, still in my school uniform, supposedly at home sick that day. The adults saw through my forged parent note, and I became the obvious choice to use as an example: the non-Catholic girl at a strict Catholic school.

The headmaster told my mum, 'We can't fault Renae's record, but we're going to make a case of this for the rest of the school.' I was expelled. The shame cut deeper than any punishment. I felt humiliated thinking about disappointing my dad. From that moment, his voice seemed to fall silent, or maybe I just couldn't hear the love in it because of the burden my heart now carried. And so I joined the hairdressing salon sooner than expected.

Hairdressing became the best thing that ever happened to me. I transformed from the shy girl with long, straight blonde hair into someone with bold, short styles and playful curls almost overnight. Sneakers gave way to stilettos, and I finally found my place.

The author as a hairdresser, aged 17

My boss quickly became a role model, teaching me lessons I still use today. She had one rule: no interruptions while working. I made sure to enforce it, especially when a persistent man kept calling the salon. Note after note, I relayed his messages to the boss, making her giggle each time. It wasn't until I met her husband, Paul, that I understood her giggles and the running joke between her and the caller. 'Tell her it's Paul' meant her husband was calling, and 'call off the bulldog' referred to my being apparently overly protective.

Those early lessons were about more than customer service; they were about leadership:

- Smile before you answer the phone; it changes everything about your voice.
- Take notes on your clients; remember the details.
- Protect your boundaries; focus when you're working.

People want to feel seen, remembered and valued. Whether in a salon chair or a boardroom, the principle is the same.

FROM HAIRCUTS TO HORIZONS: DISCOVERING MY PATH

During the second year of my apprenticeship, my parents got a divorce. Devastated and with no siblings to share the emotional load, I threw myself into work. My boss understood and took me under her wing, sharing all her knowledge and making me a skilled colour specialist. That year set me apart, though it sometimes created tension with senior stylists who resented my privileges.

When it was time for my first holiday, the girls suggested a South Pacific cruise. At just 17, I needed just my parents' written consent to travel alone; it's unreal how simple it was back then. All I needed was a passport – no need for travel insurance, visas or other paperwork. Looking back, I wonder where I found the courage. Was it bravery or youthful naivety that made me pack a suitcase and sail into the unknown?

On board, I met a charismatic pilot from Brisbane. Neither of us was prone to seasickness, which worked perfectly because we spent the first 3 days sailing through a cyclone. With most passengers and 80% of the crew bedridden, we essentially had the entire boat to ourselves.

We made the best of it, claiming a bar as our home base, mixing drinks and playing pranks on the seasick passengers curled up on deck chairs. Our antics included Frisbee competitions with whole pizzas, seeing who could fling theirs farthest out to sea without losing toppings. (That might be why pizza isn't free on cruises anymore; sorry about that.)

The highlight was our infamous Moët party. We commandeered the top level of the ship's most popular bar, armed with a blue pen we dubbed our 'symbol of power'. Entry required a contribution of a bottle of Moët & Chandon, and we'd mark participants with a bold blue 'Moët' as proof. By the end, we'd drunk the ship dry, and everyone proudly bore their blue 'tattoos'.

Coming home was more complicated than expected – my first encounter with holiday blues. Arriving at the airport I'd known my whole life, I felt disoriented, unable to navigate a place that once felt familiar. The streets of my childhood looked strange, as if the buildings had changed shape. I had changed; the holiday had transformed me into someone I didn't yet recognise. But I couldn't stay here.

Within months, Mum and I made the move to Brisbane, to the bright lights of 'Bris-Vegas'.

Every step of this chapter carried lessons that shaped the person I am today. From bias to bravery, from shame to resilience, these moments became the foundation of my journey:

- **Bias leaves bruises** – Whether in classrooms or workplaces, unchecked prejudice damages trust and potential. That experience with Sister A taught me that fairness isn't automatic; it's a deliberate choice I've carried into every leadership role.
- **Uniforms and systems simplify** – The less energy wasted on trivial choices, the more energy available for creativity and impact.
- **Customer care is leadership** – Remembering names, details and stories builds loyalty deeper than any discount ever will.
- **Adversity is a teacher** – Shame, loss and storms all carry lessons if you're willing to listen. That trip taught me the value of stepping into the unknown, even when it feels daunting.

These experiences remind me that every horizon, no matter how daunting, holds the promise of transformation. Growth often comes from the risks we take and the courage we find to become who we're meant to be.

REFLECTION QUESTIONS FOR YOU:

As you reflect on your own journey of discovery, consider these questions to uncover the lessons hidden in your story:

What 'uniforms' or systems could you create in your business to simplify decisions and free up energy?

Have you ever faced unfair bias at work? How did it shape the leader you want to be?

What was your 'first job' experience, and what lessons from it still serve you today?

When have you stepped into a bigger horizon – travel, change or risk – and how did it transform you?

Chapter 3

Human Revelations and New Beginnings

> *'Friendship ... is born at the moment when one person says to another, "What! You too? I thought I was the only one."' – C.S. Lewis*

Moving to the city felt like stepping into a foreign world. The chaos of traffic, the maze of one-way streets and the sheer scale of it all were overwhelming. But beneath the fear, there was a spark of excitement – a chance to grow into the person I was meant to be, even though I had no idea who that was yet.

I was simply following my instincts, driven by the spontaneity of youth and the rhythm of a restless heart. As I navigated the roads, I began to discover more about myself. The freedom of being behind the wheel allowed me to explore new places and push my boundaries. Each trip across the city stretched me a little further, proving I could manage more than I thought. That simple act of getting from one place to another became an initiation into self-reliance.

I secured a full-time position as a third-year hairdressing apprentice at a salon chain with 8 locations. The owners weren't hairdressers themselves but entrepreneurs who had recognised the profitability of the industry. They ran the business like a corporation, complete with sales talks, weekly targets and after-hours training seminars.

It was an education in itself. While most of us thought we were training purely in the art of hair, I began to see the business mechanics beneath it all: sales targets, reward systems, marketing tactics and the psychology of customer service. The owners weren't masters of hair, but they were masters of profit. In hindsight, they taught me an invaluable truth: no matter how creative or passionate you are, if you don't understand the numbers, your business won't last.

The environment was demanding – relentless, even. And naturally, they sent me to the hardest salon to manage: the men's salon. I didn't shy away. If anything, I leaned in. The pace was fast, the clientele particular and the expectations high. But that's where I thrived, quickly mastering the unspoken etiquette of masculine grooming while honing my ability to adapt under pressure.

The year was 1988, and Brisbane was buzzing with World Expo excitement. Our salon had the unique distinction of being the trusted spot for every undercover detective in the city – their headquarters stood right next door. As part of their dress code, detectives weren't allowed to have hair touching their ears, and with the stress of their high-pressure roles, we became their go-to retreat. We specialised in relaxing massages, and business was booming.

But business boomed more in responsibility than in our wallets. Management ran a brutal system: hit your sales targets for 2 weeks in a row, and instead of being rewarded, your budget was increased. For a teenager on apprentice wages, expected to buy new outfits weekly to maintain the salon's fashion-forward image, it was a catch-22: spend money to look successful while never quite earning enough to be comfortable.

Everything changed when I discovered my salon manager's dangerous side hustle. She was selling drugs to clients in the car park after hours. The irony wasn't lost on me – undercover detectives were our regulars. This wasn't a harmless shortcut to extra income; it was a disaster waiting to happen.

The choice before me was brutal: keep the manager's secret and protect my friendship with her, knowing I could be implicated, or step forward and protect myself while risking betrayal of someone I cared about. It wasn't just a professional decision; it was a personal betrayal. I wrestled with guilt and fear, but I knew I couldn't stay silent.

I chose to protect myself. It led to her dismissal and my unexpected promotion to salon manager at 19, suddenly responsible for a team of 5. Behind the 'success', I carried fear – fear of revenge, fear that I'd crossed an invisible line, fear that being 'the boss' at that age made me a fraud.

But it was also the first time I truly understood a lesson that would echo through my career: leadership sometimes means making the hard call, even when it comes at a personal cost.

In her place came Belle, a blonde bombshell from New Zealand who needed somewhere to stay. My flatmate and I offered her our third bedroom, and we lived and worked together, building a lifelong friendship. She appeared angelic on the outside but had a wonderfully mischievous streak – the kind of friend who could silently create chaos in an elevator and leave you to take the blame.

That friendship reminded me of the power of surrounding yourself with people who bring lightness into heavy times. In business, we need those allies – not just colleagues but companions who remind us not to take everything so seriously. A light heart can often carry us further than a heavy hand.

The author and Belle pre-dating selfies

HUMAN REVELATIONS AND NEW BEGINNINGS

We also had Mikey, our flatmate, who was the calm amidst our chaos. He made sure the rent was paid and we got to work on time, and he kept chocolate cake batter stocked in the pantry for emergency midnight baking sessions. He didn't seek the spotlight but kept the machine running, making sure details didn't slip through the cracks.

There's a bigger lesson there: every thriving household, every thriving business, needs a Mikey. In leadership, it's easy to overlook these people, but they're often the glue that holds everything together.

One of my most memorable client experiences involved a highly successful clown who also worked as a magician. During the school holidays, he was performing a children's act at our salon's shopping centre and chose me to style his hair – apparently, because our hair was the same colour. At the time, I was rocking a bright copper shade, and his wig matched perfectly. Whether that was meant as a compliment or not, I wasn't going to question it; after all, a booking is a booking.

He arrived unforgettably, riding a unicycle, and gave us his name: Urani Diot (it took me a while to see it, but you just move the space to the left). Later, he returned to erase it and provided his real name instead: Ben Dover. Since he was scheduled to perform at the centre for 2 weeks, the constant corrections left a major smudge in our appointment book, dangerously close to tearing a hole in the page. He turned out to be an absolute delight, full of humour and energy. Over the following months, he became a regular visitor, bringing fun and laughter every time he stopped by. I became his wardrobe designer, wig styler, hairdresser and test audience for new jokes and magic tricks.

Early one morning, he called urgently: he had a television appearance at 9 am, but a mishap during his fire-eating act the night before had burned off his fringe and all his facial hair. When I arrived at the salon, he smelled of burnt hair and looked pitiful.

We worked quickly to repair the damage, creating new eyebrows and ensuring he was camera-ready.

That day taught me a cornerstone of business: sometimes your role isn't about delivering the planned service; it's about solving the unplanned crisis. The clients you save in those moments become your biggest advocates. His parting line stayed with me: 'It's nice to be important but more important to be nice.'

On weekends, my flatmates and I travelled with a band. One gig was at a notoriously rough venue where the stage was surrounded by a cage, not for aesthetics but for the artists' protection. Before long, glass bottles were flying, chairs were being hurled, and fistfights erupted in shadowy corners. We knew it was time to leave when even sitting in our locked car felt unsafe.

Not every opportunity grows you; some just drain you. Discernment is part of the journey.

By the time I completed my apprenticeship at 19, I was exhausted. Managing a team while being underpaid due to my age, facing the fallout of difficult decisions, it was a turning point. When you're young and ambitious, you believe hard work will be enough. But then you discover that leadership isn't just about 'doing more'; it's about learning when to step back, assess the bigger picture and recognise when it's time to pivot.

After years of navigating the fast-paced world of the salon, I was ready for a new challenge, one that would take me far from city streets and into the open sea. My mum had left the city and returned home to Mackay to work for a cruise company, and through her, I discovered a new possibility: sailing through the Whitsundays as a way of life.

When I returned to Mackay, I stayed at Mum's house, knowing it would be hard on my dad. Seeing him so lonely, still struggling to adjust to life without her, broke my heart. But I wasn't the little girl he remembered, and that gap between us felt impossible to bridge.

His house now held only bare essentials: antique furniture, 4 of everything in crockery and cutlery, hot water turned off. In a way, this reflected his operating system for life: low overheads, simple structures, ruthless efficiency. As a young woman, I saw only sombreness. But later, I realised the same principle, 'stripping back to bare essentials', is powerful in business. Cut the fluff. Know your numbers. Keep your system lean so you can survive tough times.

My time on the ship was an incredible learning curve in extended guest care. Living alongside guests for 5 days and 4 nights was unique; there was no going home after a long day, no switching off after hours. Your crew was your family, whether you liked them or not. That was my first experience of customer care at scale: the culture is 24/7, not 9 to 5. If you want loyalty, you can't fake it.

The crew constantly changed, and when the First Stew left after 2 weeks, I was suddenly promoted from fourth to third. This is exactly how leadership opportunities show up in real life: not as a polite promotion after years of preparation but as a sudden gap that demands you step forward before you feel ready. Business moves at that pace too. If you wait until you 'feel ready', you'll never take the leap.

I bonded with the new First Stew, a tough, no-nonsense person who didn't let people in easily. Winning her over required understanding what she loved, jazz and blues, which opened my mind to a new way of life. That experience taught me that influence doesn't come from forcing your way in; it comes from listening, observing and finding shared ground. Sometimes the best way to lead is first to learn.

At the end of each week, we'd gather for crew meetings before heading to the nearest pub for happy hour. Without fail, someone would lose their balance to the 'phantom wave' – that odd sensation of rocking that hits after stepping ashore – and topple off their barstool. Every time, it sent us into fits of laughter while the rest of the bar stared, assuming we were already drunk.

I look back on this time with fondness, despite its abrupt conclusion. From the moment I stepped on board, the skipper assumed I was only there because of a favour to my mother. One day, he hurled a laundry bag at me, accusing me of slacking off and leaving work unfinished. We were on the main deck, but my assignments had been on the top deck all week, meaning the mistake he blamed me for wasn't even mine. Fed up, I walked off the ship for good that day.

Not every environment deserves your talent. Not every leader is truly leading. And knowing when to walk away is just as important as knowing when to stay and fight.

Looking back, I see how every challenge, every abrupt promotion and every difficult decision shaped the leader I am today. Growth doesn't come when things are easy; it comes when you step into the unknown and trust yourself to rise to the occasion. The people who challenge us, support us and even disappoint us all play a role in our becoming.

- **Growth comes from discomfort** – Abrupt promotions, feeling unready and complex personalities push us to evolve faster than comfort ever will.
- **Leadership is influence, not control** – True leadership comes from listening, observing and finding common ground rather than forcing your way.
- **Know when to walk away** – Sometimes the best business decision is leaving an environment that no longer supports your growth.
- **Surround yourself with the right people** – Every successful venture needs those who bring lightness, those who handle details and those who challenge you to grow.

REFLECTION QUESTIONS FOR YOU:

As you reflect on your own journey of growth and leadership, consider these questions to uncover the lessons hidden in your story:

Think of a time when you stepped into a role before you felt ready. What did you learn about yourself?

How could that experience shape the way you lead or run your business today?

Who are the 'Belles' and 'Mikeys' in your life, the people who bring lightness and keep things running smoothly?

When have you had to make a hard call that came at a personal cost? What did that teach you about leadership?

Chapter 4

Anchored in Connection: Lessons from the Sea

'Ships are safe in harbor, but that's not what ships are built for.' – John A Shedd

'A boat without port is free only until the storm breaks out!' – Mehmet Murat Ildan

After leaving the boat in Mackay, I felt untethered. Returning to Brisbane, nothing felt right; the house no longer felt like home, and I couldn't settle back into my old life. When a friend helped me secure a new opportunity in Cairns as a personal assistant to JB, who owned a rapidly growing tourism publication, I grabbed it. My friend also arranged for me to stay at JB's house. It sounded like the fresh start I desperately needed.

A girlfriend joined me for the 1,300-kilometre drive north. We drove through the day and into the night, finding ourselves on a long, desolate stretch of road, no lights, no signs of life, just the tunnel from our headlights. My friend had fallen asleep, snoring softly, while the radio's hum and cool night air from my open window kept me alert.

Then it happened. Out of nowhere, a powerful jet of water hit the windscreen and slapped me square in the face and filled my ear. Simultaneously, I heard a loud ticking that made my heart skip. Startled, I screamed. My friend jolted awake, screaming and grabbing the dashboard as I slammed on the brakes, skidding to a stop on the empty road.

For a moment, I sat in stunned silence, wiping water from my face and checking for injuries. Then it hit me, the ticking sound was a commercial irrigator spraying water across the fields and road. Realising what had happened, I burst into uncontrollable laughter. I tried to explain, but my friend just joined in, and we laughed hysterically for what felt like miles.

ANCHORED IN CONNECTION: LESSONS FROM THE SEA

Business, like road trips, is rarely linear. You'll face sudden shocks, sometimes terrifying, sometimes absurd. How you react shapes not only your experience but also impacts everyone journeying with you. Panic is contagious but so is laughter. Leaders who can reframe chaos into humour often keep morale intact when the road gets rough.

As a vibrant sunrise lit up Cairns, we passed Walsh's Pyramid, and I was captivated by the breathtaking scene. Blue mountain ranges stretched endlessly, lush green cane fields gleamed with freshness, and something stirred deeply within my soul.

It was a quiet Sunday morning when we arrived to meet JB after 10 am. We knocked persistently, wondering if we were even at the right house. Suddenly, a gruff voice called from below, and moments later, a dark, intimidating man appeared, clad only in underwear. Without a word, he opened the door, gestured us towards the lounge, then disappeared back downstairs.

He didn't ask our names or offer any explanation. We sat in the lounge of this peculiar house, one missing its entire back wall, replaced by white lattice perfectly framing a rainforest backdrop, pool and tennis court. Welcome to Cairns! While the house was extraordinary, my first interaction left me spooked, wondering what kind of place I'd entered.

That gut feeling proved right, but I wouldn't trade the 3 years of adventures in that house for anything. JB became an incredible business coach with a passion for red wine, teaching me everything about the good and the bad of both.

I naturally took on the organiser role, creating shopping lists, setting up shared budgets and ensuring everyone contributed equally. Just like Mikey had taught me. While I didn't mind shopping, I did mind watching food vanish from the fridge almost immediately. But JB often took us out for dinner multiple nights a week. We'd frequent restaurants that entered a contra deal for advertising in his magazine.

While I excelled as a personal assistant, I wasn't suited for selling advertising, which JB hoped I'd transition into. Upselling a massage or shampoo proved very different from selling ad space. I'd learned that confidence was linked to education; I'd had hours of hair training but only a brief advertising run-through.

JB taught from Dale Carnegie's *How to Win Friends and Influence People* and David Ogilvy's *Ogilvy on Advertising*, both of which are invaluable in the long term. But what I needed was solid product knowledge: ad sizes, prices, availability, page layouts, other advertisers and negotiation strategies. After visiting clients underprepared, my confidence was shattered. Looking back, with proper education, I would have excelled in selling this product.

This taught me a fundamental truth: confidence isn't built solely on enthusiasm; it's built on competence. No matter how passionate you are, without proper training and knowledge, even the most capable person will struggle to succeed.

So, I returned to sea, this time sailing from Cairns to Cape York's tip and back. Watching water shift from deep sapphire blue to vibrant cyan-green as the landscape transformed was mesmerising, an almost otherworldly experience.

I loved being back at sea, but this company also ran a tourism and hospitality training school, meaning students joined weekly, putting extra pressure on the already stretched core crew. Unfortunately, the company lacked maritime expertise and hired an ill-suited captain for this region. He was experienced but lacked the skills to navigate the Great Barrier Reef's hazards, which include 2,300 kilometres of complex reef structures, sandbanks, cays and submerged dangers, where tides, currents and weather conditions change rapidly.

ANCHORED IN CONNECTION: LESSONS FROM THE SEA

Supplies were constantly challenging. Fuel and water frequently ran low, forcing us to replenish at sea. Multiple times, water tanks were mistakenly filled through diesel lines, which was worse than simply running out of water. The result? Diesel stench and taste in urns, oil slicks in showers and frustrated guests.

The worst wasn't just chaos; it was when the captain ran us aground on the reef. Twice. The impact caused heavy listing at an alarming angle, sending panic through everyone aboard. The grinding metal on the reef sounded like the Titanic scraping ice, vibrating through our bones. Crew headed to muster stations, checking life jackets, counting passengers, waiting anxiously for evacuation orders, all with 'genuine smiles and calm, pleasing demeanour so as not to alarm guests,' as our safety handbook required. Whoever wrote that had never stood here!

Meanwhile, the deck team dived beneath to assess the damage. Twenty tense minutes later, they surfaced, assuring us the vessel was sound. We could only wait for the tide to lift us upright so we could continue.

Then there was the chef, still in his galley, desperately trying to control his words, volume and possibly his mind. He hadn't abandoned the kitchen, despite his grill being at a near right angle with flames pointing straight at him. Add 150 deconstructed lunches and pots scattered across the floor, and he was literally at boiling point. When told things were fine, he didn't take it well. The best strategy was to deliver the news and make a hasty exit.

That wasn't even the worst part; it gets worse. After the owners divorced, the ship was awarded to the wife. In a shocking act of revenge, the husband decided to have it destroyed. A bomb was planted on board, waiting for anyone desperate enough to take the money and carry out the plan; passengers and crew be damned. In a bizarre twist, the husband unknowingly hired an undercover detective to do the job. At the next island visit, all passengers were evacuated, the bomb squad was called in, and the ship was sent out to sea to disarm the explosive safely.

Leadership under pressure is revealed, not rehearsed. The captain had technical experience but lacked local expertise; a leader can be competent on paper but still fail in context. The wrong fit at the helm endangers everyone. As crew, we were asked to maintain composure externally while managing chaos internally. That's the service leadership paradox: guests don't need gritty crisis details, but they need reassurance, honesty and a plan. They rarely remember the crisis, but they will remember how you made them feel in the middle of it.

After returning to land, I worked in hospitality, an industry deeply ingrained in Cairns, given its tourism hub status. Starting as a waitress, I gradually worked my way through various departments, ultimately becoming the head manager of the lobby bar after successfully pitching an idea to the hotel that they implemented, which allowed me to build and run that bar.

I loved working in hotels, making lifelong friends. Everything fascinated me: bars, restaurants, room service and hidden behind-the-scenes hallways, which felt like stepping into a secret world. It was incredible, especially working with talented chefs, though that was rare.

Remember the rugged man in underwear who opened the door when we first went looking for JB? His name was Roy, and we became a couple. That doorway proved more than literal; it was the beginning of a life built on risk, laughter and the chaos only love and ambition conjure. He shared his dream of starting an adventure tour business, and he enlisted a friend to join him in pursuing it. That friend was me.

One night, we sat at the word processor, the kind that hummed and blinked like it was thinking harder than we were. We crafted an itinerary, formatting it into a brochure JB would print. We guessed at costs, threw numbers around and settled on prices that now make me cringe. Our business formula was more enthusiasm than expertise, but it was ours.

We hand-delivered brochures to Cairns travel agencies, and somehow it worked. Bookings trickled in, and we packed the vehicle, hitched the trailer and set off on our first Cape York trip.

The landscape was wild and ever-changing, red dust giving way to lush greenery, roads winding through silence and spectacle. It was breathtaking, unpredictable and utterly unforgiving. One night while cooking over a campfire, I burned my foot badly but suffered in silence, unwilling to disrupt the rhythm or admit vulnerability.

As the tour continued, so did the tension. My background was hotels and cruising: polished, curated, customer-first experiences. His was raw, rugged and unapologetically wild adventure. We clashed on how tours should be run, each holding fast to our respective visions. Eventually, we found peace with the divide: he'd lead expeditions; I'd become the anchor, office, home base, the quiet force behind the scenes.

He was passionate about the Cape, and I was passionate about him. I would have brought heaven to earth for him, and I tried.

Businesses are rarely born from spreadsheets; they begin with passion and possibility. Passion doesn't replace planning, but it fuels the perseverance needed to endure hard days when logic would tell you to quit. Partnerships demand clarity. Our balance worked because roles were clearly defined. Without clear roles and even task distribution, even the strongest partnerships fray.

Then I became pregnant. I hadn't realised how much I craved safety, not just physical but emotional, maternal, ancestral. When my first baby arrived, I was a nervous new mum tiptoeing through unknown territory with a heart full of love and a mind full of questions. With Roy away so often, security didn't live here. I needed something more solid than absence.

So, I went home, not just geographically but emotionally. Back to my mum, back to the woman who'd held me through my own beginnings. There was comfort in her presence, in how she moved through the kitchen, in her voice layered with memory. I needed that grounding while learning to become a mother.

It wasn't retreat; it was recalibration, a quiet decision to choose warmth over pride and connection over isolation.

I stayed with Mum in Mackay for 6 weeks after my daughter's birth. That's when JB's story took a dark turn, which rattled all of Cairns. I was on the phone with Roy when police suddenly surrounded their house, and the tactical response squad, spaced 3 feet apart, machine guns ready, entered every doorway. They asked for JB. Roy ended the call, leaving me in shocked silence.

JB had been charged as an accessory to murder and was taken to the watch house, awaiting U.S. extradition. What should have been a brief holding turned into 18 months in a place designed for overnight stays. In that time, JB did what few could: he made friends with officers and earned their trust, securing unheard-of privileges.

The last time I saw JB was at the Cairns watch house. I'd brought my baby girl to visit and give him a much-needed haircut. Officers asked if I trusted the inmate with my daughter's life as they sent my daughter in her capsule through the scanner with my cut-throat razor and scissors. Seeing excitement on his face at finally meeting her, my answer was undeniably yes. When we left, I promised I'd see him again, fully believing I'd have that chance. But U.S. troopers collected him, and that moment never came.

We'd always wondered why he celebrated 2 birthdays each year. He said it was for Alcoholics Anonymous, but that never quite added up. The whole story behind it is remarkable, but it's not mine to tell. Out of respect for him, I'll leave it unpublished here. What matters is what came after. He paid his dues. He found love. He raised a beautiful daughter with joy and pride. And then, far too soon, his life was cut short by cancer.

JB in happier times

Leaders are human: they can be brilliant teachers and deeply flawed people simultaneously. What lasts isn't titles or accolades but the influence they had on others, for better or worse.

Shortly before I visited JB in prison came an amazing surprise in my 21st birthday card. Dad always sent cards, but this one didn't contain the usual $20 or heartfelt message. Instead, it contained something unexpected: news of an older brother.

I read the letter twice, trying to process the words. In disbelief, I handed it to Roy for confirmation. 'You have an older brother. Holy shit.' Happy birthday, indeed.

As my hands trembled, a strange calm washed over me. I wanted to talk to Dad first, but he was on a job site without mobile phones, and I couldn't wait. I called Mum at work: 'Do I have a brother?' Her response: a silence so long, it confirmed everything. She'd go home and call back. That pause told me everything.

My brother was Mum's first child, born under painful circumstances. As an unmarried young woman in the 1960s, she was sent away to hide and 'pay penance' for her pregnancy. Losing him was the price she was forced to pay. He was adopted at birth, while she left that home for unwed mothers to continue life as though nothing had happened.

For a year, I struggled to forgive this hidden chapter. I was selfish in my feelings, resenting her for a decision I didn't understand, punishing her with anger until I became a mother myself. Only then did I comprehend the unimaginable emotions she'd endured.

In another universal twist, my daughter was born the following year on his 27th birthday. Mum was there, front and centre, for her arrival. Looking back, if I hadn't known the family secret and my daughter had been born on his birthday, how would Mum have coped?

On my 21st birthday, I received truth as a gift: a revelation that initially felt like a hot potato. Over the years, it became one of the greatest gifts possible, bringing understanding, healing and a deeper connection to Mum's story and knowledge of her strength.

The parallels between my brother and me were extraordinary. People constantly pointed out our resemblance. When we met, the connection was instant. Within an hour, we were finishing each other's sentences, winning Pictionary with stick figures and minds that thought alike. I could feel his injuries mirrored on opposite sides of my body. We developed oddities like ganglions simultaneously, again, on opposite ankles.

But the most surreal experience was giving him a Reiki healing session. As a rookie learning the art, I felt warm energy flowing, but I never practised again after that session. I left a sunburn-like handprint on him, lasting days, without ever touching him. That moment was both strange and powerful.

Life weaves unseen threads, and magic moments remind me how extraordinary connections can be. If you look for magic, you'll find it; if you look for sadness, you'll find that too. Nobody is happy all the time; every day has good and bad moments. Magic lies in how you handle them and with whom you share them. It's all about perspective and what you choose to focus on.

- **Confidence is built on competence, not enthusiasm alone** – Proper training and knowledge are the foundation of true confidence. Passion without preparation leads to failure.
- **Leadership under pressure reveals character** – Crisis doesn't build character; it reveals it. How you respond in chaos defines not just *your* outcome but that of everyone around you.
- **Context matters more than credentials** – Someone can be competent on paper but still be the wrong fit for your specific situation. Local knowledge and cultural fit are irreplaceable.
- **Clear roles prevent partnership friction** – Without defined responsibilities and balanced contribution, even the strongest partnerships will strain under pressure.
- **Sometimes stepping back is stepping forward** – Choosing safety and support over pride isn't retreat; it's strategic recalibration that allows you to return stronger.

REFLECTION QUESTIONS FOR YOU:

As you navigate your own journey of growth and discovery, consider these questions to uncover the lessons in your story:

Think back to a disruption in your journey. How did your reaction shape the outcome for yourself and others?

Where in your business do you need more competence-based confidence rather than relying on enthusiasm alone?

In your partnerships, are roles clearly defined and balanced? What needs clarifying?

When has stepping back into safety actually positioned you to move forward more powerfully?

Chapter 5

Forgiveness and Fortitude: Balancing Life's Trials

***'In giving birth to our babies, we may find that we give birth to new possibilities within ourselves.'* – Myla and Jon Kabat-Zinn**

She arrived after a typical 24-hour labour, almost to the minute, as if she knew the rhythm of my body and the weight of the moment. The intensity of those hours melted into awe the instant I held her: my daughter, my wondrous gift. From that first breath, I felt something ancient awaken within me: a fierce, intuitive devotion to motherhood.

It was 2 days before Christmas, and her arrival lit up the season like nothing else. Since then, I've wanted every Christmas to shimmer with her magic: more sparkle in the fairy lights, more warmth in the laughter, more meaning in the moments. She became my heartbeat that lived outside my body.

And then there was Roy. As he leaned in to meet her for the first time, something shifted in his face: a softness I'd never seen before. His usual grit gave way to a smile so full of wonder that it caught in my throat. It wasn't just pride or relief; it was reverence. In that moment, he saw not just his daughter but the fragile miracle of life itself.

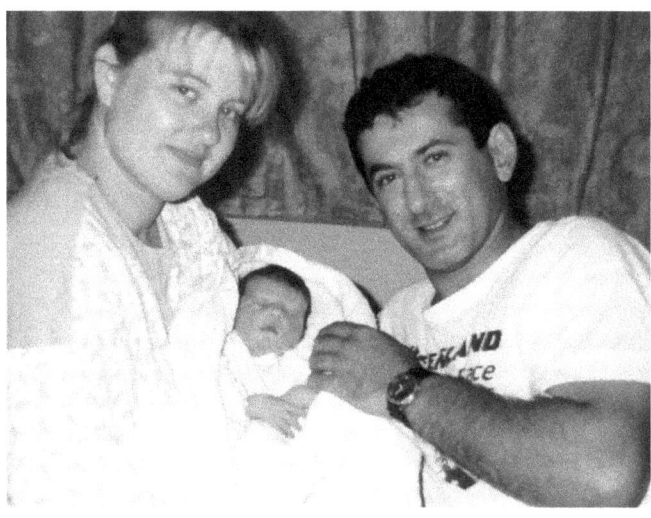

And she makes 3

I had prepared meticulously, completing a parenting course during pregnancy, driven by my belief that education is the foundation of empowerment. After all, what had I learned about being a parent? I'd only seen myself raised, and my friends had done parenting courses as subjects after I'd left school. However, no syllabus could have captured the depth of love or the clarity of purpose she brought into my life. I didn't just step into motherhood; I leapt, heart first, with passion and reverence.

What I later realised is that leadership, whether in parenting, business or life, can't be reduced to a manual. Courses provide tools, but real growth comes from presence. Just as my daughter thrived when I gave her undivided attention, so too would our budding business, our clients and eventually our team. Attention is the most fundamental form of love and the most basic form of leadership.

I wish I'd known then about 'matrescence', the complete transformation a woman undergoes becoming a mother. Just as adolescence marks the shift from childhood to adulthood, matrescence signifies the transition into motherhood, reshaping identity, relationships, priorities and sense of self. The term was introduced in the 1970s by medical anthropologist Dana Raphael, who recognised that motherhood was not merely a biological event but a rite of passage that deserved cultural recognition.

If only I had known about this concept when I needed it most, when I felt overwhelmed, raw and a little bit crazy. I might have embraced my transformation with more compassion and clarity. Discovering this term gave me language for the intensity I experienced: the passion, the purpose and the deep, aching desire to nurture not just my child but my own evolving self.

When my baby was 6 weeks old, we moved into a modest rental in a lovely neighbourhood, our business still a fledgling, learning to fly, wobbling between hope and hustle. Roy was away more often than home, and when he was home, he was usually buried in the workshop, maintaining and preparing for the next tour. My world became the baby, the baby business and the house.

I took on the role with gusto and grit, armed with a 'fake it till you make it' mindset. I had passion and purpose but a glaring lack of life skills and professional business tools. Our only vehicle was the support truck, so I had no means of escape while Roy was away.

That phrase became a quiet mantra. I now see that many entrepreneurs live in this reality: armed with more passion than polish. The courage to keep showing up, even when you don't have all the answers, builds a kind of resilience that textbooks can't teach.

Thank goodness for neighbours, and by some stroke of magic, I had one of the best. HJ had 2 children and became my friend over our competition about who could play housework music the loudest. She offered to drive me to the shops, and she became my lifeline, teaching invaluable parenting survival skills: the hands-free towel trick, how to get a child into a car seat without causing brain injury, the 'mummy' voice that meant NOW! and the upside-down rock-to-sleep method.

I wish I'd made friends with her sooner; it could have spared me the trauma of my sudsy baby sliding out of my arms onto the bathroom floor and the lifelong guilt I carry. Those early missteps can feel fatal, but what matters isn't perfection; it's recovering, learning and moving forward.

HJ introduced me to Playgroup, taking me along weekly to meet new mums. She also had diabetes that worsened with each pregnancy. One afternoon, while our kids played, HJ mentioned a fruitcake that crumbled like bricks. We weren't eating fruitcake; she was diabetic, so cake was off the menu. When I asked what she meant, she got irritated.

FORGIVENESS AND FORTITUDE: BALANCING LIFE'S TRIALS

Having overheard enough of such diabetic conversations, I realised she was having a hypo episode and needed help. I called her husband at work. As her self-conversation drifted to flying pink elephants, my instructions were to get her orange juice or a straight Coke. Not easy with 2 pregnant women in their third trimester squabbling like toddlers: one saying drink this, the other insisting she couldn't because she was diabetic. After careful negotiation, similar to the World Wrestling Entertainment, we managed it.

This lesson was paid forward years later at a school meeting when another parent started acting erratically. As the space grew larger around her, I approached, asked if she was diabetic and checked her handbag for her test kit. The horror on other parents' faces as they watched me rifle through her purse! A quick explanation and trip to the canteen for orange juice revealed the truth, and order returned.

As our business steadily grew, working from home felt like both a blessing and a curse. I often dived deep into projects, only to be interrupted by baby's demands or the never-ending mess. Amidst this chaos, I learned to navigate advertising, setting up systems that kept my diary organised for days, weeks and months ahead.

The day we bought our first computer was a significant milestone. Technology genuinely changed everything! My mum had been among the first in Mackay to use a computer; it filled a whole room and took an hour just to back up one day's data. When I achieved a perfect score on my computer assignment at school using continuous form paper printed on Mum's machine, it became a point of pride.

Before my grandfather passed away, he reflected on the enormous changes he'd seen, from horse and cart to man on the moon. He worried about rapid technological progress and its implications for my future. His words stayed with me, but rather than inspiring caution, they inspired me to learn and lead change, or risk being left behind.

Those who embrace change position themselves as leaders; those who resist it get swept away. In business, technology isn't just a tool; it's a competitive advantage that can level the playing field and open up new possibilities.

Our life became a roller coaster, going up and down, but each cycle grew bigger and better. We bought our first home, an overgrown, aged house with a huge shed, pool and big yard. We moved while I was pregnant with our son. My mum, dealing with the traumatic loss of her partner, moved in to help raise the kids and run the business.

We renovated the shed into business headquarters, creating an office away from the house. We cleared vines that had turned the house into a dark cave, discovering sunlight. We removed navy wallpaper featuring gold fleur-de-lis, painted walls to bring the home into the 21st century and built timber decks. It was an incredible adventure.

The business had a routine, except for over-organised groups who'd turn up a day early. One day, we were enjoying a lazy Sunday at home when 15 men arrived to help get things done before departure. We scrambled from Sunday into professional mode; I popped the baby boy into his cot and set my daughter up with a movie before heading to the office.

I was almost finished signing up riders when an unsettled feeling touched me. I tapped the window, signalling to Mum, 'Have you checked the baby?' No. I went back to work, but when Roy walked past, I asked again. He listened to the monitor and gave me the thumbs-up that it was silent.

FORGIVENESS AND FORTITUDE: BALANCING LIFE'S TRIALS

I don't know what happened, but suddenly it seemed like an entity entered my body, screaming silently in my head, 'NOW!' I apologised to the group and ran to check my baby. He was blue and looked frozen in the cot.

On overdrive, I grabbed him up. He wasn't there; his eyes were empty. I shook him to get his attention, then remembered we don't shake babies. I tucked him into my elbow and tried to think: 'Keep this quiet. How do you do CPR on babies? Is he alive? I need help!'

I attempted one breath, then turned to run. My yell for help came from the depths. Roy arrived in 2 steps. I handballed our baby to him and grabbed the phone; all I could think of was 000. One of the tour participants caught the baby next, calmly tipped him belly down on his forearm, tapped his back gently and walked. The other participants formed a guard of honour on the street for the ambulance.

The words, 'He's breathing; it's shallow but he's breathing,' are the best words I'd ever heard. The hospital journey felt like travelling to the moon. I remember Father Bear arriving and stopping nurses from stabbing his boy while looking for an IV line, demanding answers while I quietly watched someone else's movie play out, hoping they could fix him.

Then came 20 questions every hour for 15 hours: 'What were you doing when this happened? How did you find him? How was he placed in the cot?' All to see if 'someone' had done this deliberately. Each time, I thought hard and tried to help them find the clue they were after, unaware I was being tested.

The last time was at 2 am when I finally felt safe enough to let my baby sleep in the hospital cot. The torch shone, questions started, the baby stirred, and I lost it! Apparently, that was the correct answer: the way I broke down emotionally proved my innocence while psychologically breaking me out of frozen panic.

Roy went on tour with our heroes the next day, while the Smurf and I endured 3 days of tests, infant CPR training and learning to use the monitor attached to him for the next 2 years. He beeped with every breath, but an alarm sounded if breathing slowed below 10 breaths per minute or stopped for more than 20 seconds.

What was most interesting was how I handled this situation. While I loved my son with all my heart, I shut down from him. One evening, my mum noticed he was cooing at me while I watched TV. She nudged me: 'Look at him smiling at you.' I glanced down and agreed, 'Yes, he is.' Frustrated, she smacked me across the face, growling, 'Look at YOUR son.'

The shock broke me. I started crying and realised I'd been withholding love out of fear of losing him. That was probably the best smack I'd ever received. That painful lesson follows me: the fear of loss can make you detach from the very thing you love most.

Leadership often requires us to lean into vulnerability, not away from it. When we withdraw to protect ourselves, we rob others and ourselves of connection. The courage to love fully, even when loss is possible, is what makes great leaders.

This was a tumultuous time. Mum was dealing with grief over losing her partner, and I was grappling with constant fear surrounding my son's apnoea attack. Everything felt like it was on my shoulders. I was having vivid dreams of driving underwater with both kids, trying to save them, then spitting teeth into my palm, more teeth than could ever fit in a human mouth.

Meanwhile, the business was thriving. Roy connected with fascinating people from all walks of life, while I spent countless hours coordinating tours and handling logistics. These adventurers often called for excited chats about upcoming trips. I learned their families' names and knew when they'd arrive in Cairns. I was the customers' first contact, guiding them through the 6-18 months leading to their tour, answering every question.

However, once they set off on their adventure, I no longer existed. Roy became their guru, the legend, 'the King of the Cape'. Occasionally, one or 2 might remember my name. The generous tips and positive feedback went to the guides.

Roy was away about 252 days each year during those first fifteen years. The tiny resentments didn't arrive all at once; they crept in quietly, like weeds between cracks. I'd spend most of the year holding the fort while he was out being celebrated, toasted and tipped. When he came home, the rhythm shifted. His tiredness was physical; mine was emotional. I didn't resent the man; I resented the imbalance, the invisibility, the way my contribution was minimised, not legendary.

The business was outgrowing its identity, and our financial experts recommended formalising a company; it would be easier if we were married. With business operating well, 2 kids and a home renovation in progress, we felt we could manage marriage, too. But a traditional wedding felt overwhelming, so we decided to elope!

A childhood mate had transformed our backyard cliff into a rolling hill. As thanks, we booked him and his wife into a 5-star hotel and sent 100 roses to their room. The next morning, our celebrant arrived at their room with a champagne breakfast, asking if they'd witness a wedding while still in bathrobes. 'For whom?' they asked, as we stepped out of the elevator.

It turned into an unforgettable day. Once the initial shock wore off and the paperwork was sorted, we enjoyed a delightful breakfast before boarding a seaplane. Our destination? The pristine white sands of Vlasoff Cay, where we were to cut the wedding cake, lovingly baked and perfectly decorated by my mum.

The young family of four; inset of the wedding day

Of course, you can plan almost everything for the perfect day, except the weather. A strong gale was blowing, so the pilot suggested we head to the sheltered side of Green Island for some respite. And so we did. We spent the rest of the day soaking in the sun, swimming in the turquoise waters, sipping champagne and savouring cake. Honestly, what more could anyone need?

Shortly after our wedding, a new partner joined our business. Roy struck a deal with HG, a German friend who owned a successful motorcycle tour company in Thailand. HG needed an Australian partner to co-own land equally, and Roy offered him 50% of our business to strike a deal.

Roy had taken me to inspect a 4-acre block, but I was hesitant about purchasing a second property. To my surprise, I discovered we were not only swapping half the business but purchasing a 15-acre property, news I learned on the way to the solicitor.

FORGIVENESS AND FORTITUDE: BALANCING LIFE'S TRIALS

Owning land with an international partner came with strict conditions: the building had to be completed within a certain timeframe, and with that, Roy was headed to Cape Tribulation between tours, tinkering with his 'Meccano set'. The property was breathtaking – ocean views, mountain breezes, World Heritage rainforest – but I joined the project with angry reluctance. Our partnership with clear boundaries started to slide; not only was my work being minimised but so too was my voice.

We bought our first boat with giddy excitement that overrode common sense, taking it out the day it arrived, in 25-knot winds. The kids' first water introduction wasn't gentle lapping but towering green walls crashing over the bow. I kept one eye on Roy's face, searching for doubt; my cue to start strapping kids into life vests. Somehow, we made it through.

Cape Trib wasn't always about hard work; sometimes, we took the boat. The local river mouth launch could only be passed through at high tide. Roy pushed that window regularly, and we'd often end up dragging the boat over the sandbank like castaways. It was all adventure until we learned the estuarine creek we'd been swimming through was home to a rather large crocodile. The ancient Daintree Rainforest makes you feel safe, but you should never forget it's older than your instincts and hides dangers well.

The whirlwind continued. My brother went through a divorce, moved to Cairns and worked as our tour guide for 4 years. During that time, we grew closer; a reconnection that brought Mum immense joy but was difficult for my Dad to witness, so I kept it mostly to myself.

Eventually, Dad fell in love again and remarried, having his third daughter. Unfortunately, his new wife and I didn't see eye to eye. She kept me at arm's length; I was only permitted to speak to Dad on Sunday evenings between 6 and 7 pm. She spread falsehoods about me and never told her daughter I existed. What followed was a slow, painful estrangement from the first love of my life. There's a particular ache reserved for being erased by someone who once knew your every detail.

Panic hit me like a tidal wave one Saturday morning when a repo man showed up at our door. It felt like the first domino falling in what would become an endless cascade of chaos.

He read a document to me calmly and slowly, explaining that he was here to collect our fleet motorcycles and listed a series of registrations; it was half of our fleet. I found it difficult to understand any of the words, as though my brain had been submerged and the electrics were sparking in the worst kind of way. The sound of his voice felt distant, muffled by the rising tide of my own panic, and I could barely process what was happening.

My only thought was to call our lawyer, who, against all odds, answered his phone. He gave me a few magic words to say. The truck driver simply smiled, tipped his hat and drove away.

The root of the problem was a simple clerical error born from a system not designed for us. When we started our business, there were no commercial loans for fleets of dirt bikes. They simply didn't exist in banking yet. Our only workaround was to bundle five bikes together and classify them as a single 'car'. We had several loans, with only one digit of difference, and for months, I had been unknowingly making all payments towards only one account and failing to pay on the others. It was a sharp lesson: in business, passion alone can't protect you from paperwork. Financial literacy is non-negotiable.

Then came a major turning point. The national parks were governed by someone who didn't share our enthusiasm for dirt bikes. He'd spent years searching for a loophole to shut us down. His team raided us, copying our computer and seizing a year's worth of files. The investigation dragged on for over a year, costing us $70,000 to defend ourselves.

When we finally had our day in court, the judge took our side. We were granted the permit for the maximum period, and the judge told park officials to 'play nice'. It was a landmark case; no one had ever challenged the parks and won. However, government departments are immune to cost awards, so we had to cover all legal costs.

As we stood outside the courthouse, exhausted yet victorious, our opponent walked past with a smirk: 'See you in 3 years.' His message was clear; he planned to challenge us each renewal time, hoping to wear us down until we couldn't afford to keep fighting.

Looking back now, what a gift hindsight can be. At the time, I felt trapped in a world that didn't feel like my own, like being on a tilt-a-whirl without a seatbelt while everyone else is laughing and rejoicing in the ride. There was no pause, no escape, just the inevitability of staying on until the ride finally ended.

- **Presence is the foundation of leadership** – Whether parenting or running a business, attention is the most basic form of love and the most fundamental form of leadership. Your undivided focus creates trust and loyalty.
- **Preparation builds confidence, but adaptability saves you** – Plans rarely survive intact. Your ability to pivot and respond to unexpected crises matters more than having every detail planned perfectly.
- **Support systems are lifelines** – Neighbours, mentors and family make the difference between surviving and thriving. No leader or entrepreneur succeeds alone.
- **Fear can disconnect us from what we love most** – The fear of loss can make you detach from the very thing that matters most. Courage means leaning into vulnerability, not away from it.

- **Financial literacy is non-negotiable** – Passion and enthusiasm can't protect you from paperwork and poor financial management. Understanding your numbers is essential for long-term success.
- **Invisible contributions matter** – Behind every celebrated success are countless invisible contributions. Honour your own work, even when others don't see or acknowledge it.

REFLECTION QUESTIONS FOR YOU:

As you navigate your own journey of leadership and growth, consider these questions:

Where in your life or business are you giving your attention? How might dividing your focus be limiting your impact?

What support systems do you have in place for when unexpected crises hit? Who are your 'HJs', the people who show up with practical help?

When has fear caused you to withdraw from something or someone you care about? What would change if you leaned into vulnerability instead?

What invisible contributions are you making that deserve recognition? How can you honour your own work while building systems that make your value more visible?

Chapter 6

Knowledge Is Power: From Courtroom to Classroom

> **'Knowledge is not power, it is only potential. Applying that knowledge is power. Understanding why and when to apply that knowledge is wisdom!' – Takeda Shingen**

What's the next step when your world starts crumbling? The second major setback hit when things took a turn for the worse in Germany, and HG had to withdraw his investment from Australia. Who could blame him? By then, we hardly seemed like a stable investment. His mother had fallen sick, keeping him tied to his side of the world, and his wife had just given birth to their first child.

Meanwhile, I knew I had to find a way to keep us in the game. We had poured so much into this endeavour, with even more at stake. This wasn't just an experiment or passion project anymore; it was our livelihood. Many had doubted our decision to turn a hobby into a business, and now we'd reached the point of no return. With 2 young children in school and 2 homes on the line, failure simply wasn't an option.

I realised then that in business, blind passion isn't enough. We'd entered a world of permits, policies and fine print, a world where one overlooked clause could shut us down. If we were going to stay in the game, I had to speak that language fluently.

My solution? Enrol in a science degree at the University of Queensland. It was partly practical: applied science would give me the foundation to navigate environmental regulations. But it was also deeply personal. Having been expelled from school, I had always felt the sting of an unfinished education. This was my chance to correct that narrative.

Education became my insurance policy. When everything felt uncertain, learning gave me choices I hadn't had before. It wasn't just about the degree; it was about speaking the same language as the people making decisions that affected our future.

KNOWLEDGE IS POWER: FROM COURTROOM TO CLASSROOM

My mum had found love again and relocated to Brisbane, leaving me to navigate this chapter on my own. Realising I needed support to keep the business afloat, I hired JS, an ex-bank manager pursuing an MBA. On paper, it was perfect: he got flexible work, I got breathing room.

Training him on our operations, I handed over more responsibility than I was comfortable with, but I convinced myself it was a risk worth taking. I told myself it was delegation, the business skill everyone preaches. What I didn't see at the time was how delegation without oversight is a blindfold, and I would pay for that lesson later.

Enrolled in a hybrid program of study, I tackled coursework through the mail while preparing for residential intensives required for practical units. JS grew increasingly self-sufficient, needing less of my help, while I became deeply immersed in academic learning, a journey I hadn't realised I was craving until I was in the midst of it.

During my first residential, I made lifelong friends, including one unforgettable character: a 60-year-old, red-haired Irish barmaid. She was on the waiting list for a new hip and had a buggy allowance to get around campus, which meant she often carried everyone's books. Full of wit and charm, she was truly one of a kind, and we clicked instantly. On the second-to-last night of our 2-week residency, the quiet campus suddenly came alive as younger students returned from holidays. They moved back into dorms, disrupting the calm we'd grown to enjoy. Things escalated when they inflated a massive 12-person pool and filled it with all the hot water on campus, leaving us with nothing but icy showers. Gatton in June is bitterly cold, and freezing showers are unacceptable.

That's when 'Nanna', as we affectionately called her, stepped in. She rallied us to grab our shower kits, and together, we marched down to join the younger crowd in their makeshift hot tub. They weren't thrilled with our intrusion and made a half-hearted attempt to evict us. One particularly confident young man decided to take a bold approach, swinging his naked self between us in an effort to intimidate us into leaving.

But Nanna, completely unfazed, shot him a look and said, 'Oh, Honey, if you think that little thing is going to scare me, you've got another thing coming.' The entire pool erupted in laughter, leaving the young man mortified as he shrank away, defeated.

That night, Nanna taught me that authority comes from confidence, not intimidation. She didn't match aggression with aggression; she disarmed it with humour. I would carry that lesson into countless negotiations: sometimes the quickest way to win ground is to laugh while standing firm.

Nanna became a tremendous influence during intensive courses, guiding me as I mastered dissecting flowers, documenting my findings through detailed drawings and articulating my learnings. We tackled challenges together and achieved remarkable results as lab partners.

However, my greatest challenge came with the thought of dissecting a frog. I have an intense, almost phobic fear of green tree frogs, a fear that wasn't originally mine but my mother's, which I inadvertently inherited. I remember the exact night it began. Until that point, I'd always been comfortable handling green tree frogs. But one evening, navigating the steps of a high-block house, we found a frog on every step. Her palpable fear triggered something in me, and from that moment on, I was terrified too.

When the day arrived for frog dissection, I was relieved to find a toad on the counter instead. To my surprise, I was completely fine with it! For some reason, I'm petrified of green tree frogs but have no problem with toads. Go figure.

KNOWLEDGE IS POWER: FROM COURTROOM TO CLASSROOM

A few months later, we discovered that Nanna and I performed so well in our first residential that we received an invitation to join a research team visiting Africa to study lions at Kruger National Park. What an honour! Nanna made me promise that if she got eaten, I would bring her expensive ceramic hip back to her husband. She always had something hilarious to say.

Unfortunately, with 2 children in school and sports added to their schedule, there was no way I could leave for 6 weeks or raise the funds to join a research team. But that invitation validated something important: I belonged in this academic world, even if I'd taken an unconventional path to get there.

Following that win, I felt inspired and gained confidence in my studies. One assignment became the highlight of my academic journey. It involved studying an endemic species, and naturally, I chose the Cape Tribulation region, given our abundance of species to select from.

I selected *Gardenia actinocarpa*, a rare and endangered flowering plant. I love fragrant white flowers, which drew me to this species. According to research, it only grows in particular areas and disperses poorly due to large seeds that small animals can't carry and fruit that's unpalatable to most creatures.

I eagerly told Roy about my assignment, mentioning that it only grows near parent plants in the specific area. He insisted that it wasn't true; we had that flower growing on our Cape Tribulation property. On his next visit, he took photos for verification.

It appeared to be the same species, which meant the research was incorrect and that it wasn't endemic to the specified area. This made me think about the Southern Cassowary research I'd done; the big bird can swallow large seeds and is resistant to toxins. My assignment questioned the link between these endemic species and assessed the potential for further spread than initially thought.

I eagerly awaited my marked assignment. I was awarded 100% and received a sign-off request for publication in an academic journal. I flicked through the pages, looking for learning notes from my professor; there were none, just a tick and 100% with 'Great job' written underneath. Sometimes, the most profound discoveries occur when we challenge accepted wisdom with real-world observations.

Back home, cracks began forming. JS no longer needed my guidance and even hired an assistant without consulting me. I brushed off my unease, convincing myself I was overthinking, but small signals were building into something larger. In business, gut feelings are rarely random. They're data points our brains pick up before we consciously connect them. Ignoring them was my mistake.

With 2 years left at the University of Queensland, I decided to pursue a postgraduate degree in environmental tourism at James Cook University, meaning I could finish in one year. With that timeline secured, I had enough breathing room to enjoy school holidays with my kids, taking them on a tour of 'the worlds' and visiting Mum in Brisbane. We visited Dreamworld, Underwater World and SeaWorld, and that trip sparked a grand idea to build our own world.

A funny side note: we also attended a Crusty Demons show, and our industry friend secured a signed hat for my son. The following morning, we decided to Scotchgard (waterproof) the white hat to preserve the signatures. I sprayed every thread until it was almost wet. I lay the hat on the sink to dry and turned to see my son's horrified face and an orange glow on the wall. The hat had caught fire from a nearby tea light candle! I scooped it up and doused it in the sink. Crisis averted, I tried to convince him that a fire-blackened brim made it more authentic.

The Sunday after we returned, during a tropical downpour, Roy and I sat with my laptop, and I explained my idea to create a world. We spent the entire day dreaming in Excel, and by the end, we had a big, hairy, audacious goal (BHAG).

The school year began with new learning criteria. Meanwhile, the children started their sports regimes, which included swimming training, football and Futsal.

A few months later, Roy and JS bought a cane farm and started a company together to build the world. My name didn't appear on any documents, and I realised I'd been sold out of my own idea. While I was making academic progress, I was losing ground at home. JS had quietly rewritten the rules. My delegation, without vigilance, had turned into betrayal.

The brutal truth: in business, trust is not a system. Systems are what protect trust.

I was crushed, heartbroken and defeated, but I wasn't going to let either of those men see it. I built up my strength and stayed focused on my job at hand. We had very little time before the permit was due for renewal. However, now I was going to pay much closer attention at home. Trust was gone forever.

I started showing up at the office at various times throughout the day. That gut feeling turned into seeing things happen: documents were covered as I arrived, and conversations between JS and his assistant fell silent when I entered. It wasn't until the dominoes started to fall that we discovered he hadn't paid a tax bill in the 2 years I'd been studying.

Here we go again! I didn't give him the courtesy of 2 weeks' notice.

Beware of ex-bank managers; there's usually a reason they're 'ex', and they know a lot. When he changed our banking details, he added himself to our accounts without approval. Lesson: always strike through signature panels you're not using. Roy and I signed on the last 2 spots of page 3 and the bottom of page 5. We weren't shown page 4, which had space for 4 more signatures. No recourse there; his signature was clearly on the form.

Back at the helm, I discovered that he'd also been selling our fleet to cash buyers, banking the payments into his personal account and then transferring them back to the business as loans. Nothing looked wrong initially. We sold a fleet annually, and his dropping machines off on his way home seemed helpful. Unravelling his mess was exhausting, and we had to sit in legal mediation with this man to sort out a deal to recover what was rightfully ours.

He apologised that we'd never make it without him and genuinely wished it had worked out for all of us. I thanked him for lighting the fuse; his betrayal became my catalyst.

The winter school holidays that year were the toughest 2 weeks of my life. I was enrolled in an intensive course; my only opportunity to finish my degree within the 3-year limit. Roy was away on tour, the kids had playdates planned, I'd worked hard to get ahead in business, and I kept my phone on me constantly. Then my son broke out in chickenpox.

I felt like the worst mother in the world racing home that first day to check on him. He'd made me a sandwich wrapped in a tea towel with a glass of milk. The sweetness of his gesture undid me. I gave him a big hug, spoke a day's worth of words in 10 minutes, then bolted back to class, 9 times that week.

We all survived, and I passed, but thinking back, there's almost a black hole in my memory. Just like childbirth, we tend to gloss over the scary parts.

With the kids safely back at school, I felt relieved. We weren't required to attend lecture days, but one guest speaker representing National Parks caught my eye: the Governor. Our history was my number one complication, and while I wouldn't call him a nemesis outright, his presence stirred something in me.

Good professors understand their students, and mine knew the deeper reasons behind my enrolment. It was agreed that I could attend if I sat quietly at the back, without asking questions or making commentary. I silently listened to contradictions between his words and the reality I knew. His version of environmental stewardship was polished but selective.

It was another reminder that narratives, whether academic, political or business, always come with agendas. The real wisdom lies in recognising what's missing.

His words danced around control and care, and I found myself reflecting on the tension between protection and access. He spoke of rangers breeding snakes, some of which were released and others sold to support private initiatives. He mentioned stunning images collected over the years, hinting at a picture book he planned for retirement.

Using parks for personal projects is delicate; there are strict guidelines and permits for that work. I couldn't help wondering: were those same standards being applied across the board? It raised quiet questions about fairness, transparency and the stories we choose to tell.

The final course was built around assignment choices. I identified the real-world benefit for our business in becoming eco-certified. When I submitted my choice, the professor called me in for a chat. She told me this was the hardest choice on the list. 'I know how busy you are; would you like to revise your decision?'

I gave her my justification: the guest speaker for this course was the woman who wrote Australia's eco-certification system. What better mentor to guide me through it?

That decision became the catalyst for our business to become the world's first of its kind to gain eco-certification. With that came press releases, and I worked tirelessly to get news published everywhere I could, just before applying for our permit. It was granted without question for the next 3 years.

**Graduating James Cook University to earn
a world-first eco-certification**

With a degree and a fresh permit in hand, it was time to build this business with my hard-earned education. I had a win under my belt, fire in my belly and a new understanding of how things work in the big, imperfect world.

Education hadn't made me invincible. It had shown me just how much I didn't know and how powerful it is to admit that, then do something about it. Knowledge creates options, but applied knowledge creates power. The wisdom comes in knowing when and how to use both.

- **Knowledge creates options when everything feels uncertain** – Education became my insurance policy, giving me choices I hadn't had before. It wasn't just about the degree; it was about speaking the same language as decision-makers.
- **Trust requires systems, not just good intentions** – Delegation without oversight is dangerous. Competence without accountability can be catastrophic. Trust must be verified through structures, not just faith.
- **Gut feelings are data points your brain collects** – Those uncomfortable intuitions are rarely random. They're early warning signals that something isn't aligned. Learning to listen and act on them is crucial.
- **Vision must be fiercely protected** – Ideas are fragile. If you don't safeguard them with proper structures and documentation, others will claim or corrupt them. Protect your intellectual property like your life depends on it.
- **Authority comes from confidence, not intimidation** – True power comes from calm assurance and strategic thinking, not from trying to dominate or control through fear.
- **Sometimes betrayal becomes a catalyst** – The deepest wounds can become the fuel for your greatest transformations, if you choose to use them that way.

REFLECTION QUESTIONS FOR YOU:

As you build and protect your own vision, consider these essential questions:

Where in your life or work do you need to protect your vision more fiercely? What systems could you put in place to safeguard your ideas and contributions?

What gut feelings have you been ignoring in your business relationships? What small signals might be building into something larger?

How could education or skill development create more options in your current situation? What language do you need to learn to speak fluently in your industry?

Where are you delegating without proper oversight? How could you create systems that protect trust while still empowering others?

When has betrayal or disappointment become a catalyst for positive change in your life? How can you transform current challenges into fuel for growth?

Chapter 7

Rebuilding Trust: From Betrayal to Empowerment

'The best way to find out if you can trust somebody is to trust them.' – Ernest Hemingway

In 2006, Cairns and nearby areas were working to rebuild their tourism industry after Tropical Cyclone Larry, closely followed by Tropical Cyclone Monica. Lives were impacted, buildings destroyed, but the most substantial damage was to the natural environment that had previously drawn visitors. This led to a very quiet season with few tourists.

I remember watching weather reports as if preparing for an assignment, except this task was to save my children and protect our homes. I set alarm clocks overnight to get the latest updates. Cyclone Larry was considered the most powerful cyclone to hit Queensland in nearly a century. My parents had experienced Cyclone Althea when I was one year old, and I could feel the impact of this monstrous storm in my bones.

I completed every task on the cyclone preparedness checklist and turned the smallest, safest room in our house into a bunker. We had really large metal eskies used for refrigeration on our camping support vehicle, so I dragged them into the bunker with full intention of sealing my kids inside if that was the last thing I could do to protect them. A little overboard? Yes. But if the house started caving in, that's what I would have done. I even called Mum: 'If something goes south, come and get the kids out of the eskies!'

Preparedness became my anchor when everything else felt uncertain. The act of preparing steadies the mind and reminds us that even when we can't control outcomes, we can control how we meet them.

Cairns and our bunker location were spared major impact, but Cape Tribulation suffered significant damage. As soon as roads reopened weeks later, we made our way north to check. The further we drove, the worse the scene became. It was devastating to see the World Heritage Daintree Rainforest stripped of leaves. The mountains looked bare and wind-ravaged brown, similar to drought damage. We manoeuvred around fallen trees too big for chainsaws to cut.

We arrived at our front gate, which was still standing – a good sign! There was leaf debris as we made our slow way up the hill, but the house was exactly as we'd left it, except for a fallen plastic chair and a tray that had slid off the outdoor table. Our property, nestled between 2 mountain ridges, was unscathed, still green and leafy, while we could see damage all around us. It was as if the storm rode the ridge up, bounced over our place and slid down the opposite ridge.

Although we didn't suffer physical damage like many others, our business was impacted by a lack of bookings. People were frightened off by the media. I applied for and was accepted into a government scheme to develop a business recovery plan. We were provided with experts to work through the basics of business plans and build future-proofing ideas.

It's shocking to realise we were 16 years into the business before documenting a formal business plan. It struck me how much trust we'd placed in sheer momentum. Sixteen years without a formal plan meant we'd relied on grit and intuition but not structure.

Trust, I was learning, couldn't only be emotional; it needed scaffolding. In business, just as in relationships, systems and protections aren't about pessimism; they're what allow trust to thrive without being naive.

Part of our future-proofing strategy was creating a brand through a strategic campaign aimed at winning awards. The campaign plan was to elevate brand visibility, boost credibility and customer trust, build industry connections, open doors to partnerships and refine our strategies. This goal was stepping stone number one towards building our big, hairy, audacious moto-world dream.

I was introduced to and joined the Cairns Business Women's Club, where I met members of the Australian Institute of Management, the Cairns Chamber of Commerce and Tourism Tropical North Queensland. The door to Narnia swung wide open, and I leapt into a bright and colourful new world; a world of women doing amazing things. Some of the loneliness I'd felt lifted. I wasn't alone; there were people who thought the same things I did.

Walking into that room felt like the first deep breath I'd taken in years. Community changed everything. Isolation had made me doubt myself, but here, ambition wasn't strange or selfish; it was shared. Networks don't just open doors; they mend the loneliness that running a small business so often creates.

In 2007, I won the CBWC (Cairns Business Women's Club) Small Business Owner of the Year award and the AIM (Australian Institute of Management) Management Excellence Award for Owner Manager of the Year – Cairns, which sent Mum and me to Brisbane to represent us in the state awards. I found the scrutiny of answering questions exhilarating and discovered that entering awards was a powerful exercise in reflection, storytelling and strategic growth.

**Cairns Business Women's Club – Small
Business Owner of the Year 2007**

The process forces you to articulate your mission, measure your impact and celebrate what makes your business exceptional. It invites you to step back and see your work through fresh eyes, often revealing strengths and innovations you hadn't fully named. Engaging with judges' criteria helps refine your messaging, sharpen your value proposition and align operations with a deeper purpose. Whether you win or not, the clarity gained becomes fuel for future decisions, team pride and brand elevation.

How exciting it all was, the rare chance to buy a new dress and step into glamour that felt worlds away from the dust and dirt of this male-dominated sport. I would put myself through nerves and prep every year just for the possibility of a ticket to the ball. It was a moment to reclaim those glam skills, to do hair and makeup not for practicality but for celebration.

Seeing the company name in the newspaper and being written about by journalists was intoxicating. The adrenaline rush of public speaking, the thrill of seeing it printed, all added to the high. But beneath it all was something deeper: personal recognition.

Finally, a spotlight on the hard work I'd poured in, the invisible hours that made everything run. It was visibility, and it mattered. What surprised me most was how the award process itself became a mirror. Writing submissions forced me to see our business in sharper detail, to name our value and to own the impact we'd created.

Recognition wasn't vanity; it was renewal. It reminded me that invisible work still mattered and that telling our story was as important as doing the work itself.

As part of the prize, I was invited into a mentoring program, which quickly became the second major step towards our BHAG. I met incredible women and discovered a vibrant network of local businesses I hadn't been aware of. Some connections have lasted to this day: I still use their services, and one woman has become a valued ally. We've attended major award ceremonies together in the city, even though she's long since moved beyond the small business she started into bigger, brighter ventures.

Around that time, we finally secured council approval to move forward with the moto-world project, a long-held dream that had come to a grinding halt during the embezzlement debacle. Now it was my turn to take the reins. The damage had been deep, both professionally and personally. Putting that behind me, I chose to see the potential and follow through. We needed to find investors, rebuild trust and recover from what had felt like a devastating blow.

Instead of letting the setback define the future, I began crafting a coaching program for junior riders; a way to nurture the next generation and breathe life back into a vision nearly lost to the reckless pursuits of men chasing wealth, without heart.

I intended to build something that stood for more. I envisioned an eco-certified initiative grounded in dual-purpose values, where every element served both functional and meaningful purposes. For example, we planned to plant a tree line meeting the city's aesthetic guidelines, but I saw an opportunity to go further: grow native bush tucker along that line, inviting the local high school to participate through their agricultural program. As plants matured, they could be harvested for home economics classes, transforming the project into a living classroom rooted in sustainability, education and community connection.

We launched the initiative by signing a cooperative management plan with the Great Barrier Reef Marine Park Authority and planting 33,000 trees along the river's edge. It was a bold move designed to shield the marine park from farm runoff and create a bushland sanctuary where customers could gather, barbecue and reconnect with nature.

I returned to university for 6 months to earn a certificate in General Principles of Coaching, a stepping stone towards achieving Level 2 coaching accreditation with the sport's governing body. I did this under the careful guidance of my mentor, who would later become the mayor of Cairns. Her belief in me was steadfast, and her presence gave me the courage to keep pushing forward.

Once she took office, we began lobbying the state government for funding to support the build. A consultant flew in from Brisbane to meet with us and discuss requirements. The energy was electric; I could see light at the end of the tunnel.

After missing 2 scheduled meetings, the consultant asked to shift the conversation to email. He requested the development plan so we could 'stay on the same page.' I hesitated. That plan was like a newborn to me: fragile, precious, never far from my side. I sought my mentor's advice, and with her approval, I reluctantly hit 'send'.

Weeks went by. I checked in with my mentor weekly, then every fortnight and then monthly. I didn't want to push; she was busy running the city. Eventually, news arrived: a grant to build a motocross park was being announced. But it was only open to projects in the Great Southeast. The amount matched our request exactly. And the guide that was published online? It was my plan, almost word for word, only missing the logo.

The consultant sent to represent the state government turned out to be a private contractor, paid generously to deliver my plan to Brisbane City Council. We investigated and pushed back where we could, but since I'd sent the document with a watermark instead of a copyright notice, there was nothing we could do. It was out there now; published, claimed and repurposed.

Defeated, I packed away my research, maps and papers. I placed them in a box and tucked it deep into a dark corner where I wouldn't have to see it anymore. And just like that, the BHAG chapter closed.

In the silence that followed the outrage, I realised that betrayal doesn't have to be the end. If I couldn't trust the system, I could turn inward and learn to trust myself more deeply. Sometimes the hardest losses strip away the noise and leave you with one thing you can't lose: your own conviction.

I turned to focus on moments with my children instead of building for their future. They didn't even know they'd been waiting quietly while I chased meetings, wrote proposals and planted trees for a future they couldn't yet see. I owed them presence. I owed myself peace.

But peace didn't come easily. I quickly discovered that I'd trained my brain to run on overdrive. The gears didn't know how to idle. I'd become so accustomed to high-stakes thinking – solving, strategising, anticipating – that regular daily routine felt foreign. I couldn't just sit and watch the kettle boil. I needed tension. So, without meaning to, I started creating little dramas. Subconscious mischief. Tiny emotional fires to keep her entertained.

Her?

That's when I noticed her, the second voice in my brain. Not a figment, not a ghost but a voice. Familiar, yet separate. She was the one I asked questions of and, strangely, the one who answered. Sometimes she was wise. Sometimes she was sharp-tongued and impatient. Sometimes she was eerily calm when I was anything but.

I began to wonder: who is she? And more curiously, who am I when I'm speaking to her?

Is it madness to hear more than one voice inside your own head? Or is it a kind of sanity, a survival mechanism for women who've had to wear too many hats, hold too many truths and carry too many dreams?

I stopped trying to silence her. I started listening.

At first, it felt strange, as if I were eavesdropping on my own thoughts. But the more I leaned in, the more I realised she wasn't just noise. She was memory, instinct and intuition. She was the part of me that had been watching all along, waiting for permission to speak.

Curious, I began asking others if they had a 'someone' too, that second voice, that inner companion who answers questions before they're fully formed. Some were startled by the question, blinking as if I'd pulled back a curtain they hadn't noticed was there. But then they laughed. Every single one. Not because it was funny but because it was familiar. That laugh of recognition, of being seen in a way that's rarely spoken aloud.

We all have her, I think. Or him. Or them. That quiet council of selves shaped by experience, trauma, joy and grit. Some call it gut instinct. Others call it madness. I've come to believe it's a kind of sanity, the kind that keeps us tethered when the world spins too fast. The kind that reminds us who we are when we forget.

In a world where external trust can shatter without warning, that inner voice became my compass. She's not always kind, but she's always honest, and I can trust her. And now, I let her speak, and she's the one who nudged me to write this book. 'Let's tell the story behind the business!'

The betrayals, the stolen dreams and the moments when systems failed me; they all led to this understanding: the most reliable trust isn't placed in others. It's cultivated within. Not as a retreat from the world but as a foundation strong enough to engage with it again, wiser and more selective about where we place our faith.

That inner voice, the one we often dismiss or silence, might be the most valuable business advisor we'll ever have. She's seen every meeting, witnessed every handshake and absorbed every lesson. She knows what others can't: our patterns, our blind spots, our deepest motivations. Learning to trust her wasn't giving up on trusting others; it was building the discernment to trust more wisely.

Sometimes the greatest empowerment comes not from conquering external challenges but from making peace with the voices within that have been guiding us all along.

- **Preparedness is power in uncertainty** – The act of preparing steadies the mind and reminds us that even when we can't control outcomes, we can control how we meet them. Having systems and backup plans isn't pessimistic; it's empowering.
- **Trust needs structural scaffolding** – Systems, contracts and protections aren't signs of doubt; they're what allow trust to thrive without being naive. Document everything. Protect your intellectual property. Verify before you trust.
- **Networks heal the isolation of leadership** – Community isn't just support; it's perspective, encouragement and the shared language of ambition. Isolation makes us doubt ourselves, but the right community reminds us we're not alone in our struggles or dreams.
- **Recognition fuels resilience** – Telling your story and celebrating your achievements isn't vanity; it's renewal. The process of articulating your value and impact creates clarity that becomes fuel for future decisions.
- **The inner voice is your most reliable advisor** – That second voice, the inner companion who answers questions before they're formed, isn't madness; it's wisdom accumulated from every experience. Learning to trust this internal compass is essential for navigating a world where external trust can shatter.
- **Betrayal can become empowerment** – When systems fail and trust is broken, turning inward to strengthen self-trust isn't retreat; it's building the foundation for wiser engagement with the world.

REFLECTION QUESTIONS FOR YOU:

As you navigate your own journey of trust, betrayal and rebuilding, consider these essential questions:

When external trust has been shaken in your life – whether through betrayal, disappointment or loss – how have you rebuilt trust in yourself? What role might your own 'inner voice' play in guiding you forward?

What systems and structures could you put in place to protect your trust without becoming cynical? How can you create scaffolding that allows trust to thrive safely?

Where in your life or business do you need community to heal isolation? What networks could you join or build to find your people?

How often do you listen to that inner voice – the one that sees patterns, notices inconsistencies and guides your gut instincts? What would change if you trusted her wisdom more consistently?

What recognition or storytelling do you need to do to honour your own journey and fuel your future resilience?

Chapter 8

Adventures and Adversities: Living the Dream

> ***'We must be willing to let go of the life we have planned, so as to have the life that is waiting for us.' – Joseph Campbell***

My son was at a sleepover when he attended his first AFL game; his little friend was playing, and the excitement was contagious. He came home inspired, determined to join the season. So that's exactly what we did.

As a born and bred Queenslander, my sporting education had been firmly rooted in State of Origin Rugby. I'd never watched a game of AFL in my life. But motherhood has a way of turning you into a student of whatever your child loves. I was about to learn.

We attended training sessions, met lovely families, and slowly, my son began to open up. He was a beautiful boy, deeply sensitive to others' needs, always helpful, always kind. Ever since his near-fatal apnoea episode, he seemed to radiate something special, something soul-deep. People who were tuned in could feel it.

Unfortunately, that same sensitivity made him a target at school. The bullies saw his gentleness and mistook it for weakness. For years, they made his life difficult. As a mother, it is heartbreaking to witness your child's light dim under cruel words and exclusion. I tried teaching him to turn the other cheek, but inside, I wrestled with a different instinct: the one that wanted him to stand tall and defend himself.

Thankfully, sport gave him a new outlet. He had natural hand-eye coordination and was ambidextrous, able to kick with either foot. He took to the ball with ease. The coach was momentarily puzzled when he didn't follow the drill off his right foot, but the grin on his face said everything when the ball landed precisely where it was meant to.

Physically, my son was bigger than most boys on the team, which gave him an edge. But emotionally, he was still soft, still learning how to channel his strength. At first, he didn't care much about winning; he was just happy to be on the field.

Then, halfway through the season, he spotted one of his school bullies on the opposing team. Something clicked. He went into protection mode, not just for himself but for his teammates and their ball. He played with heart, precision and purpose. The bully hit the turf more than once, all within the rules of the game. That moment marked the end of the bullying through quiet, legal dominance on the field.

My son had found his strength and earned respect through performance. Sometimes the most powerful response to adversity isn't confrontation; it's excellence that speaks for itself.

And just like that, I was hooked. I handed over our fees in cash to 3 volunteer ladies running the club. They tucked the money into a white cloth bag at the table's centre and handwrote my receipt. As I walked away to watch my son train, I noticed the secretary reach into the bag and head to the bar, returning with 3 glasses of wine. I paused. Was that club money?

It wasn't a one-off. I didn't make a scene; I made a mental note. That year, I signed up to be a team manager.

Towards the end of the season, I asked the coach and his wife if they'd noticed anything questionable. They laughed knowingly. 'Yes, but what are you going to do, eh?' Well, I figured I'd get on the committee. And that's what the next 6 years became: a mission to make my son's club the best it could be.

When I joined the committee, no one was entirely sure how things were supposed to run. I spent that first year gathering information, documenting processes and creating a plan that made everything transparent and accessible. I couldn't let my education go to waste, and this seemed like a productive outlet for all that pent-up energy.

I rallied parents to get involved, and those who did were inspiring. We had ideas and drive, and gradually, the club grew to support 200 children. You'd think that would mean 200 volunteers, but no, we were a core group of 7 parents running the whole show.

I look back now and laugh; I must have been so bloody annoying, always pushing for structure and accountability. At the time, I thought I was just filling gaps. In hindsight, I was learning the essence of change management: gathering information, building clarity and giving people something they could trust.

What I once thought of as 'being bossy' was really an early lesson in governance and accountability, the kind of foundation that makes bigger ventures possible down the line.

Eventually, the plan evolved into something I was proud of: a living document that we could use to apply for government sporting grants. For a small club in Far North Queensland, we did pretty well. The governing body even asked if I'd consider writing a plan for all clubs. It would've been nice sideline income, but my loyalty was to my son's club, and I declined.

Over those volunteering years, I received several awards, including Manager of the Year, Volunteer of the Year at both club and league levels and a Queensland Day award from the state government. I progressed from manager to secretary to president over 2 years, but the real prize was watching those kids grow from wide-eyed little players to confident young adults.

Unexpected Queensland Day Award

Every time I saw one of those boys kick a goal, emotions would rise through my chest and spill out through my eyes. When my son's team won the U16 grand final, it was pure overflowing joy, the culmination of early mornings, sausage sizzles, muddy jerseys and quiet sacrifices made in the name of community.

When my son decided he didn't want to play anymore, I was shocked. He'd been playing hard across multiple teams, and football had woven itself into our daily lives. Every single day had football in it. I laughed when he told me, trying to mask the ache. 'But what am I going to do?' I asked. He looked at me and said, 'You don't have to quit.'

I think that was a big moment for him, admitting he was ready to step away, even knowing how deeply invested we all were. But I resigned. And I never looked back.

That chapter taught me about community, leadership, loyalty and the kind of joy that comes from showing up, week after week, for something that matters. More importantly, it taught me that sometimes the most successful leadership happens in the smallest arenas, with the least recognition but the most lasting impact.

Meanwhile, the property we'd purchased for the world sat dormant. I passed it every time I drove into town and slowly began to forget it was even ours. Maybe it was time to let go entirely, to sell it and move on. Being able to pay off our other 2 properties would be life-changing.

We secured a contract that felt like the answer to everything. On settlement day, at 4:55 pm, I got the call; the buyer's agent was requesting an extension. Roy was away on tour, fully expecting to come home to a big cheque. I felt the weight of the entire deal pressing down on my shoulders. Alone.

I rang my lawyer and made the executive decision to grant the extension but only if the buyer placed a further, non-refundable deposit paid directly into our account. When the documents arrived, I noticed the clause stating the deposit was to be held in the agent's account. No way. I wasn't signing that.

Take two arrived at 5:20 pm, and this time, the terms were right. The funds were received. He now had 7 days; long enough to dream about spending money you've never truly had and long enough to fear losing it.

Then came the blow. The businessman pulled out, discovering a policy that applied to all properties along Queensland Rivers; a blanket restriction making development impossible. We were devastated. Roy went searching for answers, visiting neighbours to see how the policy affected them. That's when he learned the truth: the policy was a mistake, intended only for the Great South East, not all rivers in Queensland.

Once again, those words 'Great South East' stole another dream. The neighbours had lost a contract the same day. We weren't alone. But in disappointment, Roy uncovered something unexpected: a big pink gem.

Before I get there, do you want to know what we did with that extra deposit? Everyone was surprised; no one ever beat that businessman. I was proud. I stood my ground, made a wise decision and scored a small win. We probably should've put it straight on the mortgages. But we didn't. We'd had time to dream, so we took our kids to Tahiti, and Mum joined us.

Exploring Tahiti's big 3 islands was like stepping into a postcard. Each place held its own magic: Tahiti pulsed with culture and colour, Moorea dazzled with emerald mountains and hidden waterfalls and Bora Bora's jagged crown jewel perched on liquid sapphire. Then came the unexpected gift: a surprise 5-star upgrade to an overwater bure (traditional Polynesian bungalow).

Waking up to gentle waves beneath us, diving straight into the lagoon from our deck, watching sunset paint the water gold was pure, indulgent bliss. For a family that had weathered so many storms, it felt like the universe whispered, 'You deserve this.'

My daughter had charted her own course early, choosing a school tech program with one clear goal: to become a deckhand, eventually skipper of big boats. Her dream was to work on super yachts sailing to exclusive waters. Tahiti wasn't just a destination; it was a mecca she'd long imagined docking in, not merely passing through.

Watching her head off alone along the dock on the other side of the world, fins in hand on her 20th birthday, was surreal. Her joy was tripled in me, not just because she was living her dream but because I had helped make it possible. I was proud of both of us.

The trials between mothers and daughters aren't always visible from the outside. We've had our share of sharp edges and soft landings, moments where I had to let go before I was ready. Providing her with this experience wasn't just a gift for her; it was a quiet triumph for me.

She slipped beneath crystal-clear waters, scuba diving with grace and determination, my beautiful mermaid. For a moment, everything aligned: the salt, the sun, the sea and the dream. She was living proof that love, when paired with fierce independence, can grow into something extraordinary.

I had planned a professional family portrait that day: iconic pinks, blues and whites against the Tahitian backdrop. But the weather didn't cooperate, and the photographer was reluctant. So, while my daughter dived, the rest of us stayed indoors and dived into duty-free instead.

As hours passed, our giggles got louder, and something shifted. Something had offended the Daddy. The mood changed, and just like that, my holiday was over. I walked on eggshells for the rest of the trip, wondering when I'd be spoken to again, trying to keep others from noticing the tension.

I quietly questioned why my fun seemed to require moderation, why my behaviour was held to a higher standard, my pleasure rationed, my voice needing to be quieter. It was as if his discomfort required a scapegoat, and I was the most convenient mirror, the one who reflected too much.

ADVENTURES AND ADVERSITIES: LIVING THE DREAM

This pattern would repeat itself in various forms throughout our marriage: moments of joy interrupted by invisible infractions, celebrations cut short by shifting moods I couldn't predict or control. Learning to navigate these emotional landmines became another skill set I developed, though I wouldn't recognise it as such for years.

Back home and back to the pink gem. The day Roy visited the neighbours, they told him their contract to sell the old pink house had fallen through. Out of curiosity, he went to see it himself. Not long after, he called to ask if I could meet him at the sand mine.

I was mid-task in the office, racing the clock before school pickup. My days ran like military operations: streamlined, efficient, no room for detours. But I went.

In front of me stood an old Queenslander, unloved for years. The yard was overgrown, cobwebs clung to corners, and broken windows gave it a haunted feel. But the bright Barbie pink was unmissable, and the stained glass in the doorway called me in like a siren.

I stepped inside and wandered through the maze of rooms in silent awe. She reeked like a homeless woman, but beneath the grime, I could see her bones: strong, graceful, full of character. A good wash and change of clothes, and she'd be a stunner.

In the centre of the house, I found Roy quietly smirking. 'What do you reckon?' he asked.

It was wonderful. It reminded me of my grandparents' house in Townsville: the same warmth, the same echoes of family laughter lingering in the walls. 'What if we move her next door to our property and live there?' he said.

After a moment's hesitation, I called my bank manager to find out how much we could spend. And just like that, we bought a house.

Usually, relocating a house takes at least 3 months. We had 6 weeks and a demolition date set. The sand mine wanted the sand under her footprint and planned to start digging on D-Day. I lobbied councillors across several districts for special permission to save her. Everyone in town knew her as 'the old pink house'. Allowing demolition would have been a tragedy.

We moved her the day before the deadline.

The Pink House

The task was enormous. The house wasn't square, had no central cut point and couldn't be split for easy transport. The main section had to be moved in one go, at sunrise, before highway traffic increased. She was wider than the bridge span, and the truck's hydraulics were pushed to the limit.

The driver had one cheek out the door and a spotter watching the front tyres to ensure the rubber didn't leave the bitumen. One degree off, and he'd bail, letting the whole thing topple into the river. As he inched across the bridge, the house wobbled like a drunk debutante in heels.

My stomach churned with every creak of timber and hiss of hydraulics. This wasn't just a building anymore; it was our Barbie dream house in real life, teetering between possibility and disaster. One wrong move and she'd tumble into the river, taking our wild hope with her.

It was madness. It was magic. And somehow, she made it.

Over the next 12 months, we scrubbed 10 years of street living off her skin, every layer of grime, every trace of neglect. We evicted bats, pythons and a whole cast of creatures best left unnamed. Her roof was replaced, bones reinforced, spirit revived. We gave her a new identity, fresh makeup, and she radiantly took up her new place with pride.

During those first weeks, we visited often, getting to know her, celebrating the victory, listening as she began to whisper. The first sign appeared when we removed broken fibro sheet remnants. Behind it was a huge, matted spider web filling the cavity. I sat back, staring up at the space, and there it was: my husband's name, clearly written in the web. Once you spotted it, you couldn't unsee it. She was speaking in a Charlotte's web.

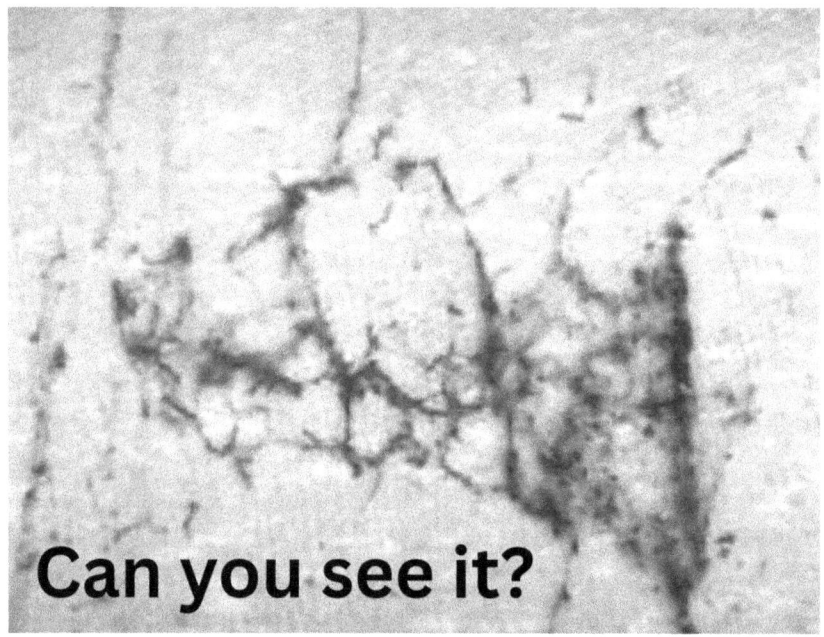

Charlotte's web

When I got a call from the previous owner's daughter, I invited her over immediately. I was hoping she could shed some light on a few finds. She told me she loved and missed the house so deeply that she'd returned at every milestone, sprinkling representative glitter in each room so the house could be part of the celebration. It was her way of honouring the joy that had once filled those walls. It took us the whole 12 months, probably more, to remove the gold 21s, the purple 18s, the silver sparkly wine glasses ... and the list goes on.

She invited a friend to the visit and brought the owner's daughter from the family before hers. There we were, 3 generations of women who had loved this house. Both girls were from families of 5 daughters. So was my mum. This house attracted women. She held their laughter, their secrets and their glitter.

ADVENTURES AND ADVERSITIES: LIVING THE DREAM

Under the layers, we found a message handwritten by the carpenter who had done a renovation. It was in Italian, a pencilled note from 70 years past. The first house sister translated it for us. He'd written the year as 1934 A, XII (*Anno Fascista* 12) – the twelfth year of fascism. A tradesman marking his work, leaving proof he'd been there and built something meant to last.

We had finally finished renovating our original home when we decided to sell it and move to the house on the river. Twenty-plus years of memories got packed into boxes. Every cupboard emptied, every drawer sorted. We didn't linger.

Mud-crabbing from your own backyard sounds idyllic, until your husband decides to check the pots at night after we've both had a few drinks. We drove the golf buggy down the ramp so he could use the headlights. There are crocodiles in that water, so I stayed in the buggy's safety while he ventured out.

I watched, giggling, as he started slipping and skating across the mossy, mud-covered concrete ramp, then lost all control and went flailing into the creek. He's not the best swimmer, built like a brick with bones that sink, so I jumped out to help, still laughing, and offered him my hand.

As he pulled himself up, I lost traction and shot past him like I was on a slip-n-slide, straight into full submersion. That's when I understood why he'd struggled; there was no grip, just slick panic. In sheer terror, I dug my knees and nails into anything I could find, clawing for escape. And still, I was laughing.

I could hear bubbles rising around me and thought, 'Well, at least I was laughing when the crocodile took me.'

Wine by candlelight turned into hot showers to scrub off creek mud and antibacterial on scratched knees, followed by a silent retreat to bed to warm up and rethink this definition of 'fun'.

Sometimes the most memorable adventures are the ones that teach us our limits while reminding us of our capacity for joy, even in the face of genuine danger.

- **Excellence speaks louder than confrontation** – My son's quiet dominance on the football field taught me that sometimes the most potent response to adversity isn't fighting back – it's performing so well that respect becomes inevitable.
- **Change requires structure, not just passion** – Those 6 years volunteering taught me that sustainable transformation happens when you document processes, create transparency and build systems people can trust. What looks like 'being bossy' is often essential leadership.
- **Small arenas create lasting impact** – The most successful leadership often happens in the smallest venues with the least recognition but the most lasting influence. Every community organisation is a training ground for larger leadership roles.
- **Trust your instincts in negotiations** – That extra deposit we secured wasn't just about the money; it was about standing firm when something didn't feel right. Gut feelings in business are usually data points your experience has already processed.
- **Joy requires protection** – Learning that my happiness could be rationed or interrupted by others' moods taught me the importance of creating internal stability that doesn't depend on external approval.
- **Preservation is sometimes more valuable than progress** – That pink house taught me that some things are worth saving simply because they hold stories, beauty and connection across generations.

REFLECTION QUESTIONS FOR YOU:

As you consider your own journey of dreams, setbacks and unexpected adventures, reflect on these questions:

Looking back at your own life, can you think of a time when a setback, side road or even messy moment gave you lessons that proved more valuable than the original goal?

Where have you found excellence to be a more powerful response than confrontation? How has performing well in challenging circumstances earned you respect?

What small arenas in your life have provided the most significant leadership training? How have community roles or volunteer positions prepared you for bigger opportunities?

When have you had to protect your joy or celebration from others' moods or reactions? What boundaries do you need to create to safeguard your happiness?

What 'pink houses' in your life, projects, relationships or dreams are worth preserving even when others might see them as outdated or impractical?

Chapter 9

Turning Challenges into Triumphs: Writing and Winning

ALWAYS RISING

'The harder the battle, the sweeter the victory.' – Les Brown

Our business is seasonal, full throttle from April to November, featuring 12-hour days from dawn to dusk. But come December, we put down our tools and extend the Christmas celebrations until March. So that's what we were doing on this particular March night: enjoying prolonged festivities, a bit too relaxed, a bit too restless.

At some point, I must've gotten bored or annoyed – hard to tell – and wandered off to chat with my horses and listen to whatever song was my favourite at that hour. I never, ever move the horses after dark. I only go for cuddles. But for some reason, that night I decided to shift them off the river and into the dam paddock.

I woke up at twilight, swallowed by the lounge, still in my day clothes, with the TV humming. I figured I'd have a shower and crawl back into bed for a lazy Sunday. Just as I crawled into bed, I realised, no phone. Memories started to trickle back. Crap. I'd left it down the paddock. So, in my cool and slightly slinky nightie, I wandered out to check on the fur babies.

Found the phone. Snuggled while I filled the trough. All was well.

Until I turned to head inside and saw a car on fire on the highway. No people. Just flames. Holy hell.

I ran to my son's room, knocked hard, told him to grab his phone. 'C'mon, we gotta go.' I dropped mine on the back stairs and jumped into the golf buggy. My Rottweiler leapt into the buggy in front of me like clockwork. My son followed, wide-eyed. Neither of us thought, 'I hope the driver's okay.' We just saw a bonfire and an oddity worth investigating.

As we reached the highway, we were joined by my daughter on the quad bike. A few cars stopped in the distance. The fire brigade arrived, did a U-turn and left. Wait; what? Strange. Then came the big black SWAT vehicle. 'Interesting,' we thought. But it drove straight past.

Then it turned into our driveway and barrelled towards us.

A man in full armour, rifle raised, was yelling, 'Where is he? Where is he? Where is he?' We were stunned. All 3 of us blurted out nonsense: 'We live here! We'll just go home!'

'Who?' He fired off the next round: 'Is there anyone else in the house?' 3 times, like a chant.

'Yes,' we said. 'Our dad. My husband. My mum. Grandma.'

'Call them out. Now.' Then he pointed to the cars: 'Go to police. Go to police. Go to police.'

My daughter peeled off down the highway on the quad. I told my son to stay off the road. We crept along in our circus buggy, the lollipop song looping in my head. Halfway there, we hit the whack-a-mole checkpoint: 4 officers popping up one at a time, yelling 'Go! Go! Go!' then ducking down again.

At the barricade, I scrambled for a leash; my dog wasn't going to take kindly to the police dogs we could now hear. We crossed 4 lanes of highway in our pyjamas, past a line of halted traffic and arrived at a crossroad packed with service vehicles. A beautiful rainbow was hanging overhead while chaos unfolded below.

The incident started with a vehicle ramming and escalated into an 11-hour armed standoff that shut down the highway in front of our house. It involved a former military reservist who fired at police and a rescue helicopter before he was fatally shot in chest-deep water near our house.

Remember how I'd randomly moved the horses the night before? It wasn't random at all; it was a blessing. The SWAT vehicle tore through both fences in the river paddock to take up position. If I hadn't moved them, my horses would've been thrown into chaos. Then came the gunfire, the fierce wind of the helicopter overhead, the kind of noise that sends animals into blind panic. But mine? They were tucked safely at the bottom of the dam, calm and clever, as if they knew the drill.

My beloved Nemo and Charisma

I stood there, watching the madness unfold and felt a strange mix of pride and disbelief. Never have I been so grateful for listening to that quiet nudge, the one that told me to break my own rule and move them after dark. It wasn't logical. It wasn't planned. It was something more profound. And in that moment, I realised just how much trust flows both ways between a woman and her animals.

The days that followed were harder still. The SES swept the grounds. Police recovered shoes and a backpack. Divers pulled an AK-47 from the river. The land felt as though it had been touched, altered, as if the soil itself had absorbed the violence and was holding its breath.

And yet, nothing touched me more than knowing a mother had lost her baby that day. My heart was broken for her.

I reached out once, gently. Eleven months passed before she responded. She asked if the family could hold a memorial on the anniversary. Of course, I said yes. And then I asked if she wanted me to walk her through the story of the day. Because if it had been my child, I would want to know every detail.

We laid wreaths at each known incident site, honouring his path with reverence and care. When we reached the river, the final wreath was released into the water; its slow drift was a quiet surrender to what could never be undone. I left the family to grieve in privacy, knowing some moments are too sacred for a stranger to witness.

That day reminded me that trauma doesn't just leave scars; it carves out new rooms you didn't know you had. And sometimes, someone else's loss brings your own life into sharper focus. The noise of the world quiets, and what remains is love; even in its absence, it's still the most powerful force we carry.

Trusting intuition isn't mystical thinking; it's listening to the data your subconscious has been collecting. That night, when I moved the horses, something in me knew. Call it instinct, pattern recognition or divine intervention, I like to call it 'the magic'. In business, we often dismiss these quiet nudges in favour of hard data. But the most successful leaders I know have learned to honour both: the spreadsheet and the gut feeling that says, 'Something's not right' or 'This is the moment.'

The world turned upside down in March 2020. That incident on our property felt like a strange prelude to what was coming. COVID-19 arrived in Australia, and everything changed overnight. For those of us in tourism, it was like watching the tide go out and not knowing if it would ever come back.

Thankfully, we had 70 acres to roam. But there's only so much mowing and gardening one can do before existential dread starts creeping in. The word 'pivot' hadn't even entered our vocabulary yet; we were still in the panic-and-bake-banana-bread phase.

Roy, however, had something else: stories. Hundreds of them. Tales from the road, the bush, the back of beyond. They'd tumble out randomly over the years, around campfires, over beers, in the middle of fixing a flat tyre. Clients had always told him, 'You should write a book.'

So, when it became clear we weren't going anywhere, I looked at him and said, 'Well, if you're trapped in the house with me, you may as well write it.'

We signed up for a 3-day author's retreat, not expecting much beyond a few scribbled anecdotes. But something clicked. The stories poured out of Roy; we laughed, big belly laughs, and I turned it into a manuscript. Sixteen weeks later, we held the first hard copy in our hands: written, edited, printed – a book born from lockdown.

The fun of writing that first book

Had we known the pandemic would stretch on for 2 years, we probably would've slowed down. But maybe that urgency was the gift. We didn't wait for perfect timing. We just started.

I was well-versed in keeping my brain busy because if I didn't, it had a habit of creating its own dramas just to stay entertained. During the pandemic, that tendency threatened to spiral. I knew I needed something meaningful to sink into, or the stillness would become unbearable.

The book became my lifeline. What started as a project for Roy quickly transformed into another catalyst for me: a whirlwind education I hadn't anticipated. Beyond those bound pages was a long line of entirely new experiences: new business systems, networking opportunities, marketing strategies and a complete upgrade of the world I thought I knew. How had I let so much time pass between educations? How had I forgotten the lessons I'd learned and slipped quietly back into the isolation of *busyness*?

How many worlds are truly out there? As you get older, you notice they're everywhere: hidden behind fear, concealed in discomfort, just beyond what feels safe. All you have to do is turn the handle on something scary and step through.

The book opened me up again. A creative spark that had been lying dormant for years ignited a warmth in my blood I hadn't realised was missing, like someone had switched the lights back on.

It's strange how easily we get lost in the busyness of building things: companies, homes, children, marriages. You become so skilled at managing logistics, solving problems and keeping wheels turning that you forget what you actually enjoy. Not what you're good at. Not what's useful. But what makes you feel alive.

You know everyone else's preferences by heart: their favourite meals, how they like to travel, what makes them feel seen, and you make it happen, often without being asked. Somewhere in that choreography of care, your own desires quietly slip to the back of the queue. There's never enough time, is there? Not for writing, painting, dreaming, whatever connects you to the part of yourself that existed before the roles took over.

When the day is filled with tasks just to keep life ticking over, creativity feels like an indulgence. Optional. Silly, even. But it's not. It's essential. Because if you don't make space for the woman inside, the one who used to play, imagine, wander, she begins to fade.

I found myself asking: 'How did I get here?' Fifty years old and somehow disconnected from the girl who used to draw horses in the margins of schoolbooks and make up stories while swinging upside down on monkey bars. It's like driving on autopilot, your hands on the wheel, your mind elsewhere, until you suddenly snap back and think, 'Wait, where am I going?'

The book was more than a project. It was a turning point. A reminder that I'm not just the operator of a business or the anchor of a family, I'm also a woman with stories to tell, instincts to follow and a creative fire that still burns, if I let it.

Creativity isn't indulgence; it's fuel. Without it, efficiency becomes emptiness. Businesses thrive when their leaders are alive inside, not just operationally competent but personally engaged with what makes them feel purposeful and energised.

Our guests have always been true adventurers: the type who chase horizons, not just itineraries. So, when COVID lockdowns kept them indoors, most didn't cancel. They simply postponed again and again, holding onto the dream of riding through Cape York as if it were a promise they'd made to themselves.

I became quite skilled at cancelling and rebooking. In the early days, each change involved about 7 separate tasks per person: emails, spreadsheets, payment adjustments and calendar reshuffles. It was a full-time job in itself. But necessity breeds innovation, and through some hard-earned lessons in systems and automation, I managed to streamline the process to just 2 clicks. What used to take hours now takes minutes.

The bookings from 2020 carried over into 2021 and then again into 2022. It created a compounding effect, like a wave building offshore. By the time borders reopened, we weren't just busy; we were inundated. Our business almost tripled, seemingly overnight.

Thankfully, we'd had time to reinvent our wheel; to upscale, refine and align our operations with growth. It wasn't just about surviving the pandemic; it was about emerging stronger, smarter and more prepared than ever.

But the landscape had changed. Where we'd once had one or 2 competitors, suddenly there were 5, maybe more. I don't know if it was job losses that pushed people into the industry we'd created so long ago or if they saw the boom and thought, 'Why not me?'

We knew better. We understood what had created the hunger for adventure: the confinement, the craving for freedom, the need to feel something real after months of isolation. And we knew it wouldn't last forever. The spike would settle. The numbers would return to normal. What mattered was whether we could hold our ground when the dust cleared.

It's such an annoying compliment to be copied: flattering in theory but frustrating in practice. Suddenly, the landscape was crowded with new operators, some experienced, some clearly winging it. Either way, the effect was the same: we had to step up. Not only to improve our product, but we also had to reassert our position. To fight the fight again, prove who we are and what this industry could be when done right.

So, armed with a book that captured our story and a fresh education that sharpened our strategy, we went back to the awards circuit. Not just for the trophies, though we've collected a few: Outdoors Queensland Gold in 2022, Queensland Tourism Awards (QTA) Bronze in 2023, Silver in 2024 and a spot on the Top 50 Small Business list. At the time of writing, we're aiming for QTA Gold in 2025.

For me, the real value is in the process. I'm the only person who's been a constant in the office. There's no one to bounce ideas off, no one to say, 'Hey, that's outdated' or 'Have you seen what others are doing?' Awards force you to look up, look around and measure yourself against the best.

I find the process less about applause and more about accountability. And yes, I remembered again to use them as an excuse to buy a dress and get glammed up once a year. But it's also about stepping outside the comfort zone, submitting your work to scrutiny and recognising where the gaps are.

If I didn't enter, I wouldn't know what progress had been made. I wouldn't know how to improve. It's easy to get stuck in your own rhythm when things are working, but leadership isn't just about doing well. It's about staying curious, staying sharp and staying ahead.

How had I forgotten this lesson and let 10 years slip by?

Somewhere in 2020, I stopped being my husband's secretary and realised I was a businesswoman in my own right. Not just the anchor behind the scenes but the strategist, the storyteller, the visionary. That shift wasn't loud or dramatic. It was quiet and internal, like a gear clicking into place.

I began to treat my mornings like mission control: establishing routines that sharpened my focus, dedicating power hours to get things done and clearing inboxes with military precision. I adopted a 'touch it once, do it now' mindset because procrastination is just fear in disguise. And I didn't have time for fear anymore.

I stopped selling the product and started selling the story: the grit, the legacy, the wild beauty of Cape York. I planned, I dreamed, I went. And I realised that if I wanted to keep growing, I needed to surround myself with people who inspired me, not just professionally but personally.

If you don't know them, find them. If they intimidate you, lean in. The people around you shape your trajectory, and I've built an extended team that reflects the kind of leader I want to be: curious, capable and unafraid to evolve.

Imposter syndrome still knocks, but I've realised it's a signpost, not a stop sign. It means I'm stretching, reaching into places I haven't yet mastered. And mastery only comes by leaning in.

My grandfather once worried about how I'd keep pace with the future. I think about that often, and I've chosen my answer: not with dread but with curiosity.

The transformation from 'helper' to 'leader' rarely happens overnight. It's a series of small decisions to step into your own authority, to trust your instincts and to stop waiting for permission. The pandemic forced many of us to examine not just what we do but who we are when everything familiar falls away.

Crisis has a way of revealing what matters most. For some, it's security. For others, it's connection. For me, it was creativity and autonomy. The moment I stopped asking 'What should I do?' and started asking 'What do I want to create?' everything changed. The business grew, but more importantly, I grew. And when leaders grow, everything else follows.

- **Instinct is strategy in disguise** – That quiet nudge, the one that tells you to move the horses or take an unexpected path, is often your subconscious processing patterns your rational mind hasn't recognised yet. In business, honouring both data and intuition creates the most powerful decision-making.
- **Creativity fuels resilience and innovation** – When leaders stay connected to what makes them feel alive, businesses gain energy and vision. Creativity isn't indulgence; it's fuel that prevents efficiency from becoming emptiness and operations from becoming soul-crushing routine.
- **Crisis reveals identity and priorities** – The pandemic forced us to examine not just what we do but who we are when everything familiar falls away. The businesses that thrived weren't just the ones that pivoted fastest but the ones led by people who knew their core purpose.
- **Identity is claimed quietly through daily choices** – Transformation rarely arrives with fanfare. The shift from 'helper' to 'leader', from 'secretary' to 'strategist' happens

through consistent choices to step into your own authority rather than waiting for permission.
- **Competition is validation, not threat** – Being copied is an annoying compliment that signals you've built something worth replicating. Instead of retreating, use it as motivation to refine your positioning and demonstrate what excellence looks like in your industry.
- **Systems thinking transforms chaos into opportunity** – When demand tripled, we didn't just work harder, we worked smarter. The investment in systems and automation during quiet times paid dividends when growth exploded.

REFLECTION QUESTIONS FOR YOU:

As you navigate your own journey of growth, identity and leadership, consider these essential questions:

When the world tips on its head – whether through crisis, competition or change – do you freeze, push harder or lean into curiosity and reinvention? What would change if you chose curiosity as your default response?

What creative spark have you been ignoring or relegating to 'someday' status? How might reconnecting with what makes you feel alive transform your leadership and business energy?

Where are you still playing the role of 'helper' when you could be stepping into 'leader'? What daily choices could help you claim your authority more fully?

What instincts or gut feelings have you been dismissing in favour of 'hard data'? How could you create space to honour both analytical and intuitive decision-making?

If competition entered your space tomorrow, would you be ready to demonstrate what excellence looks like? What stories, systems or strategies do you need to develop to stand confidently in your expertise?

Chapter 10

Love, Loss and Legacy: Finding Meaning in the Journey

'Grief is the price we pay for love.' – Queen Elizabeth II

What truly makes the journey worthwhile? Is it the business we create, the bucket list we tick off or the loves we lose along the way? Sometimes I wonder if we're here to endure deep pain just so we can recognise joy when it finally shows up. Or perhaps it's about learning to live with the losses, to walk through trauma and emerge on the other side with a deeper version of ourselves. The kind that doesn't just survive but evolves.

At what point in our human journey should we begin speaking like this, with weight, balance and honesty? How do we navigate our days knowing everything can change in a moment? What truly matters, and what gives each day significance?

I lost a wonderful friend and business mentor far too soon to breast cancer. Her laugh was unmistakable, a sound that filled the room before she even stepped in. She was a bright light, the kind of woman who could find naughty humour in even the most polished, professional setting and make it feel like a gift. She named her breasts; they were unapologetically hers, part of her identity, her presence, her power. She loved them both until one went rogue.

The battle that followed was brutal. The treatment changed her shape, her energy, her sense of self. She lost the girls, and I can only imagine how devastating that was, not just physically but emotionally. I felt helpless. Until I realised I could still bring her magic.

She was both my personal and professional travel agent. We exchanged emails and phone calls every week, and I always looked forward to the packets she sent, the ones that marked an upcoming adventure. That's when I knew what to do. If she couldn't travel, I'd bring the world to her.

I planned a tour from A to Z. I started with Armenia and created a dream holiday, sending a packet with a brochure, tour itinerary, room details and a postcard. I tucked in a small gift from the region; something tactile, something real. I mapped out the entire alphabet and enlisted friends to help send packets from different locations around the state, so she'd never know where they were coming from.

Each week, a new destination arrived anonymously: Bermuda, Cuba, Dominica, Estonia. A new escape. A new reminder that she was still part of the world, even if her body couldn't take her there.

We made it all the way to N. I'd already bought the present for O – Oman – and written the letter about the silver trade. But my heart broke when I had to rewrite that letter as her eulogy. She suspected I was the one who started it. A few people found out because I'd involved them in helping with the packets. But nobody ever confirmed it to her. Nobody wanted to spoil the magic.

I'd bought her a silver necklace, intricate, meaningful, chosen with love. I wrestled with whether to send it with her or keep it. In the end, I decided it was meant to stay with me. I made a vow: I would travel, and I would take her with me.

I wore the necklace to Tahiti, and she came with me. In a tiny black pearl shop, a woman behind the counter approached me, her English broken but her eyes kind. She pointed to my necklace and asked, 'Does it tune?'

I gently tinkled the bell. She laughed and said, 'Your angel with the white hair has the most amazing laugh. She laughs every time she hears that.'

I stood there, stunned, tears immediately filling my eyes. And so it was confirmed: the magic hadn't ended, it had simply changed form.

Last year, I travelled to Egypt to celebrate my birthday because she had always said she wanted to cruise 'De Nile' for her 50th. It took me an additional 4 years to make it, but 'Tink' and I got there in the end. After Tahiti, I named the necklace, 'Tink'; it spreads fairy dust everywhere I go.

Sometimes leadership means creating meaning from pain. When we can't fix what's broken, we can still choose how to honour it. That alphabet journey showed me that the most meaningful gifts aren't always grand gestures; they're the steady, small acts of love that quietly affirm, 'You matter,' time and time again.

When my father divorced his second wife, something unexpected happened: our relationship began to blossom once more. We found common ground in the unfamiliar terrain of parenting adult children, navigating the shifting boundaries of independence, respect and letting go. His daughter, nestled between my 2 in age, was in her mid-20s, and although he was in his early 70s, he often took my lead.

It was a curious reversal, one I accepted without resistance, using the very lessons he'd taught me as our new guide and conversation starter. It was a healthy clarification of all I had suspected, and it was deeply rewarding.

Not long after, he was diagnosed with terminal prostate cancer. Six months, they said. I still believe the emotional suffering, loneliness and quiet depression he'd endured played a role in the diagnosis. He'd always joked that he was only good for 17 years; both of his marriages had lasted exactly that long. And it's only now, writing this book, that I realise he may have meant me too. I left him to go to the city when I was 17.

The shock of his diagnosis stirred something in me, that familiar instinct to make magic out of pain. I turned my focus to him. Christmases became special again, and he was there, present, softened.

My dad was of the breed that believed there was nothing overseas worth chasing. Australia was the best country in the world, and we had more than enough space and beauty to explore. He'd chastise me for taking the kids travelling, insisting I should be pouring that money into the mortgage. 'Pay it off first,' he'd say. 'Then you can splurge.'

He was a minimalist before the word was a trend. Twice, after divorce, I watched him strip the house back to basics: 4 knives, 4 forks, 4 plates. The hot water system was turned off again. Comfort was replaced with timber antiques and the furnishings of yesteryear. It wasn't austerity. It was his way of reclaiming control, of returning to something solid and known.

That first Christmas, I changed tactics. Instead of asking Dad where he'd like to go overseas, a question he'd always brushed off with patriotic disdain, I asked, 'If there were something outside of Australia you'd want to see, what would it be?'

He paused, thoughtful. Then said, 'The Great Wall of China.'

Of course. He'd always had a soft spot for Chinese food, culture and especially the history of Chinese migration during Queensland's gold rush. So I went straight to the computer, and by some stroke of luck, there was a flight and package deal for 7 nights in Beijing. I printed the booking confirmation and a passport application, wrapped them together and handed them to him with a grin: 'Merry Christmas. We're going to China.'

He looked at me like a child caught between shock, panic and pure excitement. Over the next 3 months, that feeling grew. He checked in with his doctor, scheduled chemo around our travel dates and started to lean into the idea.

I bought him a proper suitcase, a real one, not the cardboard port he'd kept in the cupboard for decades, and gave it to him for his birthday. It was symbolic. We were going somewhere new, and he was coming with me.

From the moment we boarded the plane, my dad became someone else. Or maybe he became more himself. He laughed louder. Had more stamina. Ate cake for breakfast. We got lost in alleyways, and he didn't flinch. Locals took sneaky photos of the blue-eyed man with silver hair, and he basked in the attention like a rock star.

Who was this man? It was my absolute pleasure to get to know him.

He got to see my organisational skills in action, the itineraries, the bookings, the quiet logistics that made chaos feel seamless. And I got to see his curiosity bloom in a place he'd once dismissed. We grew more appreciative of each other's quirks. We made it all the way back to the beginning, before the mortgages, the arguments, the distance. Everything else melted away.

On the flight home from China, Dad turned to me and said, 'You know what I've always wanted to see? Cherry blossom trees.' So the next year, we did just that. We chased petals across Japan, letting beauty guide us.

LOVE, LOSS AND LEGACY: FINDING MEANING IN THE JOURNEY

The Great Wall of China with Dad

Reframing the question changed everything. Instead of asking what he didn't want (overseas travel), I asked what he might want if barriers were removed. It opened a door that had been locked for decades. In business and relationships, sometimes we're asking the wrong questions. The magic happens when we shift from 'Why not?' to 'What if?'

He survived 9 years and 39 rounds of chemo, not because the odds were in his favour but because he refused to be a cancer patient. He filled his head with the mindset of an elite athlete. Bought walking shoes. Walked to the pool every day. Swam a kilometre like it was a ritual.

And with the pool came 2 unlikely lifelines: the Old Boys and the Italian Mob swimming groups that met every day and socialised. They welcomed him in, gave him nicknames, shared stories and baked goodies, and slowly, the isolation and depression that had once clung to him began to fade.

He had something to live for. Every single day.

Travel became his compass. He started ticking off destinations like a man on a mission. He even went on a trip with one of the Old Boys, without me. I was so proud. It meant he'd found his own rhythm again.

On our last trip to Bali, I surprised him with a first-class seat. He giggled like a schoolboy, eyes wide with wonder, completely unsure what to do with the oversized seat and the tiny bowl of nuts. So, he did the only thing that made sense: he smiled. That kind of smile that said, 'I'm still here. And I'm loving every minute of it.'

I'd made my way to his place so we could celebrate his fortieth chemo treatment together. I brought cupcakes and party hats, a small, silly gesture to mark a monumental milestone. We planned to share them with the nurses he'd grown close to over the past 8 years, the ones who knew his humour, his stubbornness, his stories.

But when Dad came out from his routine pre-chemo chat with the doctor, he walked straight past me. His face looked like it had taken a punch. The drive home was quiet. The last round hadn't touched the tumours. The doctor had decided to pull the pin. This was it; the final leg. He led the emotions. We didn't cry; we just swallowed the pain with graceful calm.

It was around the same time Queensland passed the Voluntary Assisted Dying laws in 2023. Dad told me plainly that's what he wanted. If he couldn't care for himself, he didn't want to be here. He would not be a burden. He'd battled long and hard: stayed in his home, mowed his own lawns, swam laps, baked cakes and biscuits and cracked jokes. He held on to his dignity and routine until the last 3 months.

I was in Egypt when he collapsed and was sent home from the hospital with digital access to support services. But Dad didn't do digital. He waited for nurses who never came. He stopped eating, not out of pain but disinterest. Two weeks later, I brought him home to my place, kicking and screaming. He packed a suitcase for 7 days; it was his way of staying in control.

To access Queensland's Voluntary Assisted Dying program, Dad had to meet strict eligibility criteria: he needed to be diagnosed with an advanced, progressive condition expected to cause death within 12 months, be experiencing intolerable suffering and retain full decision-making capacity. The process required 2 formal requests, 2 independent medical assessments and a final written declaration. There were waiting periods, paperwork and a dedicated support team. It wasn't quick, and it wasn't simple. But it was compassionate. It gave Dad a sense of independence in a time when everything else felt beyond his control.

We tried every trick in the book to get him to eat, something, anything, but he faded away, slowly and stubbornly, until he was skeletal. His light left his laughter, but the twinkle stayed in those beautiful blue eyes.

I organised for his siblings to visit, and he rallied with such effort that they left believing he'd be around for months yet. He held court, cracked jokes and sat upright in his chair like a man still in charge of his story.

But the Monday after they left, he decided it was his day.

All the training I'd done with the Voluntary Assisted Dying team vanished from my mind. I had once smirked at the information brochure inside the locked box; it looked like a children's picture book, all soft colours and rounded fonts. But that day, I couldn't read a single word or understand the pictures. My heart was breaking. My brain was on the fritz. But he was calm. Brave. Determined. And that's what I had to be too.

I couldn't do this alone. I called the nurse, and thankfully, she came to our side. She spoke gently with him, asked the questions she needed to ask, and he answered with clarity and conviction. He was ready.

He sat up in bed, raised the glass and said, 'Well, last drinks,' before swallowing it all down. We got him comfy. I climbed in beside him, curled into the space that had always felt like home. My sister was on the phone. He'd made the decision so quickly that she hadn't had time to arrive. I think, as she was so young, he didn't want to burden her with this finality. He was always protecting someone.

He looked out the window at the trees, eyes following something I couldn't see. Then he pointed and said, 'Ooo, butterfly.' I squinted, searching the branches. 'What kind?' I asked.

He never answered. The last word my dad said was, 'Butterfly.'

The absolute perfection of that word. It was no accident. It was a confirmation of love for my sister.

Dad had always been an avid watcher of birds and butterflies, not in the sense of a twitcher but in the quiet, daily reverence of their song, colour and graceful movement. Nature was his companion. He had a few favourites, humble, familiar and full of personality, and now, they've been visiting me in the most extraordinary ways.

I've had birds in my office before. I've had baby bats, frogs and even a snake slither across my foot. But nothing like this. Nothing with intention.

The morning after Dad passed, a fledgling sunbird perched on my computer screen at sunrise, waiting for me. It didn't panic or flinch. It simply sat, watching. When I cupped it gently in my hands, it stayed calm and curious. When I stepped outside, it flew, strong and fast, straight towards the sky.

Since then, a kamikaze peewee knocks on the window every afternoon around 2 pm, like clockwork; Dad drank coffee at that time of the afternoon. And the clearest sign of all: the willy wagtail. He comes straight in, perches on the curtain rail and hops about until I say, 'Good morning.' Then he sings a few notes, just enough to say, 'Hi, I'm here,' and flies out to start his day. Almost every day since. That's 8 months so far.

These are Dad's top 3: the sunbird, the peewee and the willy wagtail. Nature itself is conspiring to remind me he hasn't gone far.

The weeks following Dad's death were a strange mix of grief and grace. The practical tasks, memorial arrangements, the legal paperwork and the clearing of his possessions kept me moving. But it was in the quiet moments, when the birds appeared, that I felt his presence most strongly.

Grief, I've learned, isn't linear. It doesn't follow a schedule or respect deadlines. It arrives uninvited, at inconvenient moments and demands attention. But it also carries memories that shimmer with new meaning, connections that feel deeper and appreciation for moments that once felt ordinary.

Leading through loss, whether personal or professional, requires a different kind of strength. It's not the strength that powers through obstacles or forces solutions. It's the strength that holds space for pain while still choosing hope. The strength that honours what's been lost while remaining open to what might still come.

In the months that followed, I found myself returning to the lessons Dad and I had discovered together. The power of reframing questions. The importance of finding something to live for every single day. The way travel, literal or metaphorical, can crack us open to new versions of ourselves.

But perhaps the most important lesson was about legacy. Dad's legacy wasn't in the things he left behind, the house, the savings, the tangible assets. It was in the transformation he'd undergone in those final years and how that transformation had changed me too.

He'd taught me that it's never too late to say yes to adventure. That dignity isn't about avoiding difficulty; it's about choosing how you meet it. That love expresses itself in countless ways, including through the willingness to let go when holding on would cause more pain.

The business world often talks about legacy in terms of empire-building, succession planning and market dominance. But real legacy is more intimate than that. It's the courage you model, the kindness you show, the way you help others discover parts of themselves they didn't know existed.

My friend's legacy lived in every destination packet I sent, in the laughter that followed me to Tahiti, in the reminder that love finds ways to transcend physical limitations. Dad's legacy lives in the birds that visit, in the trips I'll continue to take with his spirit as my companion and in the way I will try to approach questions with curiosity instead of assumptions.

- **Leadership sometimes means creating meaning from pain** – When we can't fix what's broken, we can still choose how to honour it. The most meaningful gifts aren't always grand gestures; they're small, consistent acts of love that say 'you matter' over and over again.
- **Reframing questions unlocks possibility** – Instead of asking what someone doesn't want, ask what they might wish to do if barriers were removed. In business and relationships, shifting from 'Why not?' to 'What if?' opens doors that seemed permanently locked.
- **Purpose creates resilience in the face of endings** – Dad survived 9 years beyond his prognosis, not because of medical miracles but because he found something to live

for every single day. Having a reason to get up transforms both the quantity and quality of our time.
- **Dignity is about choice, not circumstance** – True dignity isn't avoiding difficulty, it's choosing how you meet it. Control isn't about outcomes; it's about maintaining grace and how we respond to what we cannot change.
- **Legacy lives in transformation, not accumulation** – Real legacy isn't in the things we build or leave behind; it's in how we help others discover parts of themselves they didn't know existed and the courage we model along the way.
- **Grief and grace can coexist** – Loss carries gifts if we're willing to receive them: memories that shimmer with new meaning, connections that feel deeper, appreciation for moments that once felt ordinary.

REFLECTION QUESTIONS FOR YOU:

As you consider your own journey of love, loss and the legacy you're creating, reflect on these essential questions:

How can you create meaning, resilience and legacy in your relationships, community or leadership journey – even in the face of inevitable loss or change?

What questions are you asking that might be keeping doors locked? How could you reframe them to open new possibilities?

What gives you something to live for every single day? How can you cultivate more of those elements in your life and business?

When you think about your legacy, what transformation do you want to create in others? What courage do you want to model?

How do you honour those you've lost while remaining open to new forms of connection and meaning? What signs of continued presence do you notice when you're paying attention?

In your leadership roles, how do you hold space for both grief and grace? How do you support others through their own experiences of loss and transformation?

Chapter 11

Rebuilding in Real Time: The Aftermath and the Anchor

'You won't be the same person who walked into the storm. That's the point of the storm.' – Haruki Murakami

I love to travel. I'm in the industry – I study it every day, it's always in my face, so why wouldn't I? I'm not sure what I love more: the planning or the payoff. Maybe it's the anticipation, the spreadsheets, the thrill of locking in a deal. Or perhaps it's the moment you step off the plane and realise you've made it happen.

It all started when I won a trip to Disneyland, all expenses paid for 2 or partially for 4. I chose the latter. I was going to take my kids, then 6 and 8, and my mum, who'd never seen snow. We were going to tie that in, a proper winter adventure.

When I was growing up, every Sunday at 6 pm, our family would tune in to Disneyland on television. It was a tradition, and everyone I knew would talk about it on Monday at school. The music, the magic, the promise of adventure, that one hour made our week special. I think that's where my love of travel first started.

My grandmother passed away suddenly but peacefully, with a cup of tea in her hand and a smile on her face, while watching Disneyland. If there's a perfect way to go, that might be it: joy on the screen, warmth in your hands and peace in your heart.

I was about 7 when I made my parents promise to take me there someday. It was a childhood vow, sealed with wide eyes and big dreams. And now, decades later, I had the chance to follow through, not just for myself but for my mum and her grandchildren. It was time to turn that promise into a passport stamp.

Our business is seasonal, so summer in the southern hemisphere and winter in the northern hemisphere is our window. That's when we can sneak away without things falling apart. Roy didn't like the cold; that's partly why he left Victorian winters to live in Cairns.

REBUILDING IN REAL TIME: THE AFTERMATH AND THE ANCHOR

Someone had to stay behind and look after the business, as well as feed the pets. So, it was settled. Flights, plans, dreams.

Then came September 11.

I got the call in the middle of the night: 'Turn on the television.' We sat in shock, wondering if this was real, grieving like the rest of the world. But a decision had to be made. The company offered us a delay, wait a year and see what happens or choose another Disney location. Mum and I discussed the logistics, both feeling fear. This was her first big adventure outside Australia.

My gut told me: If we leave it, it might be too late. The kids were the perfect age for a trip to Disneyland. And yes, we were frightened to travel to France without the comfort of English. But fear wasn't going to win. So, we went to Paris. And it was magic.

Fear will always murmur, 'Not yet.' But opportunity favours the bold. In moments when the world feels uncertain, the timing seems off and others retreat, it's courage that transforms hesitation into a powerful advantage. Disneyland Paris feels like a fairy tale. Sleeping Beauty's Castle rises like a storybook image come to life, with cobbled lanes and pastel turrets that make you forget the world outside. Paris itself was a dream. Croissants in the morning, snowflakes on our jackets and the kind of awe that only comes when you step into a place you've only admired in pictures.

Mum gasped and giggled with bright childlike eyes when she saw her first snow. The kids saw wonder, and it filled my heart to overflowing. And I saw what happens when you choose adventure over hesitation: magic multiplies.

There's something magic about planning a trip for someone you love. Not just booking flights or choosing destinations but curating an experience that will live in their memory long after the suitcase is unpacked. In 2023, when my grandson was old enough to dream, I knew it was time. I'd been quietly saving for years, and now the moment had arrived: Disneyland. Not just any Disneyland: Anaheim, California. The original. The one that started it all.

This time, it wasn't just about ticking off a bucket list. It was about leaving a legacy, about watching wonder unfold in the eyes of my grandson, who still believes in magic. I planned the trip with precision, having spent 2 years on spreadsheets, bookings and route debates.

Five of us would start in Los Angeles, spend a week in an Airbnb and explore Disneyland and the city. Then we'd hire an RV and cruise the coast: Santa Monica, Santa Barbara, Santa Cruz, San Francisco. A white Christmas in Lake Tahoe. And finally, Las Vegas, the adult Disneyland. I left it for last, just in case we blew the budget.

My grandson and daughter at Disneyland California

REBUILDING IN REAL TIME: THE AFTERMATH AND THE ANCHOR

Planning was my domain. Execution was theirs. I knew better than to expect enthusiasm during the prep phase; no one wanted to talk logistics or choose between 2 incredible sights in advance. But on the day? Suddenly, everyone had an opinion.

I'd anticipated this, so I built in buffer days. 'Here's the itinerary,' I said. 'Here's how far we need to drive to make the next booking. The rest is up to you.' One night, we slept in a McDonald's car park because the RV park was full. Another night, I forget what went wrong, but I was reminded, again, that winging it isn't my style.

This is a fundamental leadership principle I've carried into business: plan meticulously but leave room for others to contribute. Provide people with structure, then grant them autonomy within that framework. Control the bones, but let others add the flesh.

Despite the hiccups, the trip was brilliant. I got to spend uninterrupted time with my grandson, close, curious, full of joy. The adults had their moments, of course. But we managed. We laughed. We explored. We made memories.

And somehow, we left a trail of strange weather behind us. Freak waves hit the coast after we left the Santas. An avalanche swept through Tahoe. Snow fell in the desert. It felt like we'd stirred something up.

But nothing compared to what was happening back home.

We'd timed the trip carefully, low season, before the wet season normally starts. My 79-year-old mum was holding the fort with a skeleton crew. Then Cyclone Jasper appeared. The team prepped for wind, locked down and braced. The cyclone passed with minor flooding. No major damage. Relief.

Then it stalled.

For 4 days, it hovered over Cairns, dumping record-breaking rain. Some areas recorded 2,000 mm in 5 days. By the time the city realised this wasn't a typical flood, it was too late. My mum was alone, flooded in, watching it all unfold.

From our luxury RV park in Las Vegas, we watched the disaster unfold on our phones. Horror. Helplessness. Guilt. We were told to enjoy our holiday. We tried. But that rock sat heavily in our stomachs.

Distance during a crisis is its own special torture. You're watching your life unravel through a screen, powerless to help, torn between the joy you've planned and the devastation you can't prevent. It's a reminder that even the best-laid plans are subject to forces beyond our control.

Ten days later, we drove into a different world. We'd left the property pristine: 4 boys had spent 4 days mowing, gardening, whipper-snipping, getting ahead so we could relax. What we returned to was devastation.

I stopped counting losses at $500,000. I couldn't bear to know more.

But what I do know is this: people showed up. A whole football team of volunteers appeared to help. By the time we got home, the pool was blue, the floors were clean, and the walls were washed. All that remained was the mountain of ruined furniture, mattresses, electronics and everything left on ground level. Sorting through it was heartbreaking. But the thought of those people coming to help? That still brings me to tears.

One image stays with me. The water came in fast, up to a metre, moving at 40 kilometres an hour. A double-door fridge freezer floated 500 metres down the driveway, across 4 lanes of highway and landed in the neighbour's yard. Inside, a bottle of Veuve Clicquot, perfectly intact in its box. Water is strange like that; it will move telegraph poles from garden edges but leave pine-bark mulch behind.

We lost a fleet of bikes. A brand-new Land Cruiser with just 1,800 kilometres on the clock. Written off.

So, I did the only thing I could think of. I threw a New Year's Eve party for the volunteers. We drank that champagne and partied for 24 hours straight. We needed the release. We needed each other and a bloody good time.

In a crisis, people matter more than strategy. Community is the real safety net. All the insurance policies and emergency plans in the world can't replace human connection when the waters rise.

The weeks that followed were a masterclass in rebuilding, not just physically but emotionally and strategically. Every day brought decisions. What to replace? What to upgrade? What to let go? It was exhausting but oddly liberating. When everything you *thought* you needed is suddenly gone, you discover what you *actually* need.

The business had to keep running. Bookings were coming in for the season ahead, guests were counting on us, and the machinery of operations couldn't stop simply because our personal world had been upended. I found myself operating in 2 distinct modes: grief and pragmatism, often within the same hour.

This is where years of systems thinking paid dividends. Because I'd documented processes and built redundancies, because I'd trained my team and streamlined operations, we could function even when the physical infrastructure was compromised. The intellectual property, the client relationships, the operational knowledge, these intangible assets proved more valuable than any piece of equipment.

But the emotional toll was significant. There's a particular exhaustion that comes from making a thousand small decisions while your heart is still catching up to your new reality. Insurance assessors, contractors, suppliers, everyone needed answers I didn't have the energy to give.

That's when I learned another crucial lesson: delegate the decisions you don't need to make personally. Not everything requires your genius or your anxiety. Some things just need someone competent who cares about the outcome.

I also discovered the importance of ritual in times of upheaval. That New Year's Eve party wasn't just about celebration; it was about marking the end of one chapter and the beginning of another. It was about transforming trauma into gratitude, loss into connection.

The volunteers who showed up weren't just helping us clean up; they were participating in something larger. They were demonstrating that community isn't just about the good times, it's about showing up when the waters literally and figuratively rise.

Six months later, we weren't just rebuilt, we were better. The new systems were more efficient. The updated equipment was more reliable. The refined processes were more robust. We'd used the disruption as an opportunity to upgrade everything we'd been making do with for years.

But more than that, we'd learned something fundamental about resilience. It's not about avoiding storms; it's about building the capacity to weather them and emerge stronger. It's about creating deep enough roots in the community that when the winds come, you don't blow away.

The experience also changed how I think about travel and adventure. Yes, we were away during the crisis, and yes, there was guilt about that timing. But we were also reminded that experiences are the one thing no flood can wash away. The memories we made with my adult children and my grandson – the wonder in his eyes, the connections we forged – these remain intact regardless of what happens to the physical world.

There's wisdom in the old saying about putting all your eggs in one basket. But I'd learned something more nuanced: diversify your sources of meaning. Build a life where joy comes from multiple streams, relationships, experiences, creativity, service and growth. When one stream runs dry or gets contaminated, the others can sustain you.

The flood taught us that we were more resilient than we'd known, but it also showed us the limits of self-reliance. The night we stood in that champagne-soaked yard, toasting with people who'd spent their holiday helping us rebuild, I understood something fundamental about leadership and life.

We're only as strong as the community we've built around us. Success isn't just about what you achieve; it's about who shows up when your achievements get washed away.

Fear whispers, 'Wait,' but opportunity belongs to the brave; when the world feels unsafe and timing seems wrong, that's precisely when courage becomes a competitive advantage. The best adventures often begin with the scariest decisions.

- **Great leaders plan meticulously but leave room for contribution** – Give people structure, then grant them freedom within that framework. Control the bones, but let others add the flesh. This creates ownership and adaptability simultaneously.
- **Community is the real safety net** – In a crisis, people matter more than strategy. All the insurance policies and emergency plans in the world can't replace human connection when the waters rise.

- **Systems thinking pays dividends during disruption** – When physical infrastructure fails, intellectual property and operational knowledge become your most valuable assets. Document processes and build redundancies before you need them.
- **Resilience is about capacity, not avoidance** – It's not about preventing storms; it's about building the capacity to weather them and emerge stronger. Create deep enough roots in the community that when the winds come, you don't blow away.
- **Diversify your sources of meaning** – Build a life where joy comes from multiple streams: relationships, experiences, creativity, service, growth. When one stream runs dry, the others can sustain you.

REFLECTION QUESTIONS FOR YOU:

As you consider your own journey through challenges and rebuilding, reflect on these essential questions:

When fear, setbacks or crises threaten your business or leadership journey, how can you stay true to yourself and lean on both preparation and people to keep moving forward?

What systems and redundancies do you need to build now, before crisis hits? How can you create intellectual property and operational knowledge that survives physical disruption?

Who would show up if your world got turned upside down? How are you cultivating the kind of community that demonstrates care through action, not just words?

How do you balance meticulous planning with leaving room for others to contribute? Where might you be over-controlling instead of empowering?

What sources of meaning and joy have you built into your life? If one stream dried up tomorrow, what others would sustain you?

When everything you thought you needed suddenly disappears, what do you discover you actually need? How might current losses be opportunities for strategic upgrades?

Chapter 12

The Beginning of a New Chapter

'The cave you fear to enter holds the treasure you seek.'
– Joseph Campbell

There's a moment in every business owner's journey when the shine dulls. The thing you once loved, the thing you built with your bare hands and sleepless nights, begins to feel heavy. It's not that the passion is gone; it's that the weight of responsibility settles in. The constant problem-solving. The endless demands. The realisation that growth comes with friction, and success comes with its own set of problems you never anticipated.

I've watched it happen to so many who started around the same time we did. They began full of fire: passionate, generous and unstoppable. And then slowly, almost invisibly, they hardened. Cynicism took root. They grew tired. They stopped seeing people as individuals and started seeing them as transactions. They lost the spark that made them magnetic in the first place.

But some of us find an alternative approach. Not because we're immune to the weight but because we've learned how to carry it differently. We've discovered practices and philosophies that keep us connected, inspired and moving forward, even when the path gets steep and the storms roll in.

That's what this chapter is about: the principles that helped me navigate 35 years of building something meaningful and the ones I believe can help you create whatever success you're called to build.

The First Lesson: Connection with Boundaries

Before I was a business owner, I was a hairdresser. Hairdressing taught me the art of connection; how to ask questions that mattered, how to listen not just to words but to pauses, how to remember the details of people's lives and reflect them back with care. That skill became the foundation of how I build relationships in business.

Everyone matters: customers, colleagues, suppliers and the stranger in the checkout line. Respect travels. It creates ripples that extend far beyond the immediate transaction. When you treat people as whole human beings rather than functions in your business ecosystem, something shifts. They remember. They reciprocate. They become part of your story.

But being an only child also taught me something equally important: the necessity of boundaries. I learned that solitude is medicine, not loneliness. That it's okay to step back, to replenish, to know when to walk away from situations that drain rather than energise.

Business needs both a deep connection and firm boundaries. Relationships and renewal. The capacity to give fully while protecting what matters most. This isn't a contradiction; it's sophistication. It's understanding that sustainable leadership requires both an open heart and a strong spine.

Think about the relationships that have sustained you through difficult seasons. They're likely the ones where you felt truly seen and simultaneously respected, where your boundaries were honoured, not challenged, where connection happened within a framework of mutual respect.

That's what I strive to create in every business relationship, from the guest who books a single tour to the suppliers who've worked with us for decades. Connection doesn't mean becoming best friends with everyone. It means treating each person as worthy of your attention, your honesty and your care.

The Second Lesson: Emotional Safety as Strategy

Most businesses chase profit, process and performance. All necessary. However, what's often missing is emotional safety: the environment where people feel secure enough to be honest, creative, vulnerable and fully present.

For me, emotional safety isn't soft; it's strategic. It's what allows innovation to flourish. It's what keeps customers loyal through mistakes and changes. It's what prevents resentment from eroding culture. It's what makes people stay, not just physically but emotionally invested in what you're building together.

Emotional safety starts with the leader. When my son nearly died from apnoea, when my father was battling cancer, when we lost half a million dollars to a flood, in each crisis, I had to decide whether to shut down emotionally or remain open. Whether to become bitter or stay curious. Whether to blame or to learn.

Each time, I chose openness, not because it was easy but because it was necessary. Because emotional safety begins with modelling the behaviour you want to see. If you want others to be honest about mistakes, you have to be honest about yours. If you want creativity and innovation, you have to create space for failure and learning.

This doesn't mean being a pushover or accepting unacceptable behaviour. It means creating clear expectations within a psychologically safe environment. It means addressing issues directly but with compassion. It means understanding that behind challenging behaviour is often fear, a feeling of being overwhelmed or having unmet needs.

When people feel emotionally safe, extraordinary things happen. They tell you the truth about what's working and what isn't. They bring forward ideas that might seem crazy but could be brilliant. They forgive mistakes and work together to find solutions. They become invested in outcomes rather than just completing tasks.

The Third Lesson: Business as Sacred Relationships

I've never liked the word 'customer'. It feels transactional, cold and disposable, as if people exist solely to generate revenue. I prefer to think in terms of relationships, not in the boundary-less way that blurs professionalism but in the way that says, 'I see you. You matter. Your story is part of my story.'

This philosophy shaped how I approach every interaction. Instead of processing bookings, I was connecting with adventurers. Instead of handling complaints, I was solving problems for people I genuinely cared about. Instead of marketing to demographics, I was sharing stories that might inspire someone to take their own brave step.

Relationship in business looks like, for example, remembering that Sarah's husband just retired, and this trip is their celebration. Or asking about Tom's recovery after his accident. It looks like celebrating milestones and supporting people through grief. It means asking questions that reach beyond the invoice to touch the human experience.

And here's what happens when you operate from relationship rather than transaction: people reciprocate. They become advocates, not just customers. They refer friends and family because they trust you with people they love. They stay loyal through challenges because they feel valued, not just served.

This approach sustained us through every crisis: the legal battles, the competition and the natural disasters – because we weren't just rebuilding a business; we were honouring relationships. People backed us because they felt connected to our story, invested in our success.

But a relationship also means accountability. It means delivering what you promise, communicating honestly when things go wrong and always operating from integrity. It means treating people's trust as the precious resource it is.

The Fourth Lesson: Visibility as Leadership

For years, I stayed in the background. I ran the systems, solved the problems and ensured everything worked seamlessly. But I didn't let myself be seen. Visibility felt risky, vulnerable, exposing. What if I wasn't smart enough, polished enough, successful enough to deserve attention?

Then I realised something significant: visibility isn't vanity. It's how we claim space. It's how we show others what's possible. It's how we lead by example, rather than by instruction.

When I finally started speaking up, writing, sharing stories, telling the complicated truth about being a woman in business, something shifted. People didn't connect with a polished facade; they connected with the realness. They saw their own struggles reflected in mine and found the courage to keep going.

That's when I understood that visibility is not just about being seen; it's about giving others permission to rise. When we share our authentic journeys, the failures alongside the successes, the fear alongside the courage, we normalise the full spectrum of human experience in leadership.

Your story matters, not because it's perfect but because it's real. Every challenge you've overcome, every lesson you've learned, every moment of growth – these become stepping stones for others following similar paths.

Visibility requires courage, yes. But it also requires responsibility. When you step into leadership visibility, you're accepting the role of guide, mentor and example. You're saying that your experience has value beyond your own success and that your journey can serve as a beacon for others.

This is why I wrote this book. Not because my path is the only path but because sharing it honestly might help someone else navigate their own journey with more confidence, more support, more understanding that they're not alone.

The Fifth Lesson: Success Through Story and Transformation

I don't just want to build a business. I want to create something that lasts beyond the spreadsheets and contracts, something that outlives the physical structures and bank balances. I want to leave a legacy that lives in the hearts and minds of people who were touched by our work.

Success, I've learned, is built through story and transformation: how we make sense of change, how we honour what matters, how we pass along not just knowledge but wisdom.

Every guest who returns from Cape York carries stories. They've seen ancient landscapes, challenged their limits and connected with something larger than their daily concerns. But more than that, they've proven to themselves that they're capable of more than they knew. That transformation ripples outward into their families, their work and their communities.

That's success. Not the monuments we build but the lives we touch. Not the wealth we accumulate but the courage we inspire. Not the problems we solve but the strength we help others discover within themselves.

The same is true for every interaction in your business, every relationship you build, every challenge you help someone overcome. You're not just providing a service or product; you're participating in someone's story of growth, discovery and possibility.

This perspective changes everything. It transforms daily tasks into opportunities for impact. It turns customer service into soul service. It makes every difficult day worthwhile because you remember the larger purpose driving your work.

Today Is the First Day of Your Next Chapter

If there's one thing I've learned through 35 years of building dreams, weathering storms and starting again, it's this: business isn't just about strategy. It's about humanity. It's about how we connect, how we protect what matters, how we grow through challenges and how we pass along what we've learned.

We're living in a time of unprecedented change, overwhelming information and constant pressure to do more, be more, achieve more. But what if the secret isn't adding more to your life? What if it's about distilling down to what truly matters, then doing that with extraordinary care and intention?

What if success isn't about reaching some distant finish line but about showing up fully to each day's opportunities for connection, service and growth?

What if leadership isn't about having all the answers but about asking better questions and creating space for others to find their own wisdom?

These aren't just philosophical questions; they're practical ones that can reshape how you approach every aspect of your business and life.

Looking back over the chapters of this book, I see patterns emerge. The moments of greatest growth came not from success but from challenge. The deepest satisfaction came not from achievement but from service. The strongest foundations were built not on certainty but on values that could withstand uncertainty.

Every setback became a setup for something better when approached with curiosity rather than bitterness. Every betrayal taught lessons about trust and systems that made future relationships stronger. Every loss revealed love in new forms and taught me to appreciate what remains.

This is the paradox of building something meaningful: the very things that threaten to break you often become the experiences that make you wise, resilient and deeply human.

The Invitation Forward

Your story isn't finished. The chapter you're living right now, whether it feels like triumph or struggle, is part of a larger narrative that's still being written. Every choice you make, every risk you take, every person you impact is adding to a legacy that will outlive you.

But legacy isn't something that happens automatically. It's created intentionally, through daily decisions to show up with integrity, courage and care. It's built through the accumulation of small acts of service, moments of authentic connection and choices to do the right thing even when it's difficult.

You don't have to build an empire to leave a legacy. You don't have to become famous to make a difference. You don't have to be perfect to be powerful. You just have to be real, consistent and committed to growth, both for yourself and for others.

The world needs what you have to offer. Not a sanitised, perfected version of your gifts but the real thing, complete with scars, stories and the wisdom that comes from having walked through fire and chosen to keep walking.

Whatever you're building – a business, a team, a family, a community, a new version of yourself – you don't have to do it alone. The strongest leaders are those who understand that success is a team sport, that support multiplies strength and that community transforms individual achievements into collective transformation.

A Personal Invitation

As this book ends and your next chapter begins, I want to extend a personal invitation. If something in these pages has resonated with you, if you've seen your own struggles reflected in mine, if you've felt inspired to take your own brave step, if you're ready to build something meaningful, I'd love to be part of your journey.

Beyond these pages, I've created ways to walk alongside those who want to build legacies of their own, businesses and lives that last, that matter, that feel like home. Through mentoring, community building and shared experiences, we can transform individual dreams into a collective reality.

Because here's what I know after all these years: the path is always easier when you're not walking it alone. The vision is always clearer when you're surrounded by others who see what you see. Courage is always stronger when a community supports it.

Your story matters. Your vision matters. Your dream of building something meaningful in this world matters. And it doesn't have to remain just a dream.

THE BEGINNING OF A NEW CHAPTER

This moment, right now, as you're reading these words, this is your invitation to begin. Not tomorrow, not when conditions are perfect, not when you feel ready. Today. Now. With exactly the resources, knowledge and courage you have in this moment.

Because the truth is, you'll never feel completely ready. The path will never be completely clear. The timing will never be perfect. But your desire to create something meaningful? That's already perfect. That's already enough. That's already everything you need to take the first step.

The cave you fear to enter, the challenge you've been avoiding, the risk you've been postponing, the dream you've been protecting; it holds the treasure you seek. Not gold or fame or easy answers but something infinitely more valuable: the discovery of who you become when you stop waiting for permission and start creating the legacy only you can build.

Your next chapter is waiting. The pen is in your hand. And I believe in what you're about to write.

FINAL REFLECTION QUESTIONS:

What chapter of your story are you ready to begin writing?

How can you create more emotional safety in your current relationships and leadership roles?

Where have you been hiding your authentic story, and how might sharing it serve others?

What legacy do you want to leave in the hearts and minds of people you encounter?

What first step will you take today towards building something that matters?

Afterword

With Gratitude for Every Step

As I close these final pages, I find myself looking back, not just at the stories I've shared but at the people and moments that gave them meaning. To every person who has been part of my journey: thank you.

Thank you to those who saw the spark of a vision before it became a flame. Your belief gave me the courage to keep going.

Thank you to those who brought joy, connection and celebration. You gifted me memories I carry like treasures: reminders of what's possible when we lead with heart and live with purpose.

And thank you to those who delivered the hard lessons: the challenges, the criticism, the closed doors. You may never know it, but you sharpened my resilience. You gave me grit, clarity and the resolve to rise stronger. I've turned those lessons into something meaningful, and for that, I am deeply grateful.

This book is a tribute to the journey, as well as to the people. Every milestone I've reached carries the fingerprints of others: family, friends, mentors, clients, critics and team. And while I've walked many paths in solitude, I've never walked them truly alone.

To you, dear reader: thank you for walking this journey with me. If these stories have sparked something in you, softened a struggle or reminded you of your own strength, then this book has done its job. Your legacy is waiting to be written, one meaningful step at a time.

Success isn't built in grand gestures; it's built in the quiet moments, the hard choices and the setbacks we make successful. I'm proud of mine, and I hope you'll be proud of yours.

With all my heart,

Anissa Renae xx

About the Author

Renae is a visionary entrepreneur and advocate for ethical tourism, with decades of experience shaping customer-centric experiences in Tropical North Queensland and beyond. As a founding director of Cape York Motorcycle Adventures, she has championed sustainable practices, immersive storytelling and strategic partnerships that elevate guest satisfaction and regional prosperity.

Her leadership style is characterised by relational fluency, strategic thinking and a deep-seated respect for the people and places that have shaped her journey. Known for transforming challenging moments into opportunities for growth and loyalty, Renae has built a career rooted in integrity, innovation and impact.

Beyond tourism, Renae is a creative force exploring entrepreneurship through design, coaching and digital innovation. She blends storytelling with visual artistry, develops mobile-first experiences and has recently created an app that invites users to co-create their own narratives. Her work celebrates legacy, honouring the past, embracing the present and inspiring others to shape their future with intention.

Her memoir, *Always Rising*, is a testament to the power of resilience, adaptability and the quiet work of building something that lasts, values she has lived and applied throughout her entrepreneurial journey. The book reflects her belief that every experience, positive or painful, can be transformed into something meaningful and powerful.

Whether mentoring small business owners or crafting immersive business experiences, Renae leads with purpose. Her mission is clear: to help others recognise that their stories are their most valuable assets and that a true legacy is built not through recognition but through the setbacks we turn into successes.

Connect with Renae to explore how your own story can become the foundation of your legacy.

As a young woman finding my way, I crossed the ditch to Brisbane, Australia and walked into a Barber's Shoppe in Chermside Shopping Centre. I was greeted with an unforgettable, 'Oh no!! Not another blonde!!' That moment marked the beginning of a lifelong friendship.

Over the years, I've witnessed Renae's incredible resilience: how she faces challenges head-on with grace and determination. Her leadership style is magnetic, effortlessly connecting with people and building relationships that truly matter. She has shown up authentically in our friendship, always with kindness, humour and unwavering support. Watching her grow, adapt and inspire others has been a privilege.

Renae, you've left an indelible mark on my life, and I know your story will do the same for so many others.

Luv U my friend now and always. ♡
Michelle Burton, New Zealand

Being drawn toward such a vivacious personality was inevitable some 30+ years ago. Although I mourn the loss of my hair now, it was the vehicle that led to our paths crossing way back when. There was always a level of professionalism, pride and earnest commitment to providing a customer experience that struck a chord with me, given my sales background. The combination of all those elements meant I was a returning customer to the hairdresser I knew as Renae.

To then have the opportunity to share a house with Renae and Belle was not only just a series of mischievous teenage (always legal) adventures, but there is no better way to learn about someone and their makeup.

N.B. Don't share a washing machine with hairdressers and not expect your laundry to be covered in hair!

Not only did I learn that it's Anissa Renae, but there was always an inner determination and attitude to follow through on decisions, plans and beliefs, all the while searching for more within her. This search for more meant that, as the situation required, destiny decided that friendship became 100s, even 1000s, of kilometres apart, as the girls headed north to a new chapter.

Despite years without contact, things pick up where they left off when we chat, and AR announces she co-owns a business, CYMCA. The unwavering drive, focus, time and effort required to create, promote and build a trailblazing, market-leading and multi-tourism award-winning eco-certified business is a credit to and validation of those characteristics I witnessed firsthand.

Every successful business is built on a cornerstone of excellence in all aspects and a vision to provide a service people love and talk about. AR has a proven track record, and now that she has chosen to share her extensive experience in her own words, it testifies to her willingness to share and inspire growth in others. This won't be a textbook; instead, it's an honest and relatable story of the challenges and experiences of a long-time friend I'm grateful for.

Friend (noun): a person known well to another and regarded with liking, affection and loyalty.

Don Rice, Brisbane, QLD AUS

My Friend Renae

I absolutely love her. We first connected through Facebook – a story in itself – and it was through her that I found my forever Friesian horse. From there, our friendship blossomed. Together, we created our tradition of 'merry unbirthdays' and Mad Hatter tea parties, simply to bring more joy into our days. That joy has carried into countless moments we've shared, each one unforgettable. Her ability to tell a funny story is unmatched – she has a way of lifting spirits and filling a room with laughter.

What I admire most about Renae is how she shows up – always. Whether it's for her family, friends or the wider community, her loyalty and resilience never waver. She is the backbone of her family business, holding everything together with strength, love and determination. You can always count on her.

Above all, it's Renae's deep family values and the heart she puts into everything she does that make her truly exceptional. Lots of love, Mima. xxx

Jemima Batt-Andersson, Table Top, NSW AUS

When Renae opened her gates in 2018 and welcomed my old horse onto her property, I thought I was just finding a place for him to live. What I actually found was something I'd been missing since moving north: a community and a woman at the centre of it who quietly held it all together.

Over the years, I've watched that house stay steady while life swept over it in waves: difficult characters, a siege, floods both small and biblical, injured horses and panicked owners. But alongside the chaos came campfires, tailgates, BBQs and baby showers. Those moments stitched our little community together as much as the challenges did.

When the cyclone tore through in 2023, it was no surprise to see the community rally for Renae and the Kundas. People came together to try to get the house back into shape and shield them from the worst of the devastation that had struck while they were overseas, a true testament to the gratitude and loyalty she inspires. And while others might have stayed down, Renae rose again and again, facing family heartbreaks and health crises, all while helping to steer Cape York Motorcycles.

Renae has shown me, and everyone around her, that resilience doesn't mean being unshaken. It means being knocked down, bruised, sometimes grieving, but still rising, still building, still showing up with generosity and grit. She proves that leadership isn't about titles or speeches, but about the way you hold people together when life falls apart.

I've been lucky enough to witness that up close, and it's left an imprint on me.

Her story matters, not just for women in business but for anyone who has ever faced setbacks and wondered if they could keep going. Renae shows that you can – and that you can rise stronger.

Speaker Bio: Anissa Renae

Business Pioneer / Storytelling Mentor / Advocate for Women in Business

For over 35 years, Anissa Renae has been a trailblazer in the adventure tourism industry, building a six-figure business from scratch and quietly shaping one of Australia's most iconic eco-certified motorcycle tour companies. As the "woman behind the man" in a male-dominated field, Renae's contributions often went unnoticed—until she decided to step out of the shadows and into her own light.

Today, Renae is on a mission to empower women to do the same. Through her courses, mentorship, and speaking engagements, she helps women uncover the power of their personal stories, build magnetic brands, and create businesses that inspire and thrive. Her journey from setbacks to success is a testament to resilience, adaptability, and courage.

Speaking Topics:
- Turning Life Lessons into Business Success
- Building Confidence as a Female Leader
- Making a Big Impact in Everyday Ways

Renae's authentic, relatable style leaves audiences inspired to rise, lead, and own their unique stories.

welcome@anissarenae.com

Your Story is Your Superpower

Turn It into Your Greatest Asset!

After 35 years of being the invisible force behind someone else's success, I finally found a way to step into my own light.

And now I help women like you do the same.

Reclaim your voice, your vision, and your worth, without guilt or apology.

Join the 6-week transformational course to unlock the power you forgot.

Unleash Your Potential!

Anissa Renae

Get Your FREE PDF!

welcome@anissarenae.com

Your Journey Doesn't End Here. It's Just Beginning.

You've just walked through a story of resilience, of rising from the ashes, and of turning setbacks into success. You've seen how every challenge, no matter how daunting, holds the seed of an incredible transformation. That same power to rise, to rebuild, and to redefine your future lives within you, too.

Your story is your most valuable asset. But what if you had a guide to help you harness its power? What if you had a community to lift you up and a proven path to follow?

This is your invitation to take the next step.

Introducing "Always Rising" Your 6-Week Transformation

If this book was the spark, the course is the fire.

I have created an immersive 6-week journey designed to help you move from inspiration to action. This is not just another program; it's a mentorship, a community, and a step-by-step blueprint for building a life and business that truly lasts.

Together, over six weeks, we will:
- Build Unshakeable Resilience.
- Step Into Your Power: Find your voice.
- Overcome Your Biggest Setbacks.
- Create Your Lasting Legacy.

This journey is delivered directly to you through our dedicated app, with bite-sized lessons, practical exercises, and a supportive community of fellow risers who understand your path. It's designed for the busy woman, the quiet builder, and the determined entrepreneur who is ready to make a real, lasting change.

You've finished the book. You've felt the connection. Now, it's time to apply these lessons directly to your own life.

Don't let this moment of inspiration fade. The world needs your story, your strength, and your leadership. You have everything it takes to rise stronger than ever before. Let's do it together.

Your transformation is waiting.

Download the app and enroll in the "Always Rising" course today.

Join the movement. Start your rise.

welcome@anissarenae.com *Anissa Renae*

Notes

ALWAYS RISING

NOTES

www.ingramcontent.com/pod-product-compliance
Lightning Source LLC
Chambersburg PA
CBHW040108100526
44584CB00029BA/3899